Maps
Globes
Graphs

Level C

Writer
Henry Billings

Marian Gregory
Teacher
San Luis Coastal Unified School District
San Luis Obispo, California

Gloria Sesso
Supervisor of Social Studies
Half Hollow Hills School District
Dix Hills, New York

Norman McRae, Ph.D.
Former Director of Fine Arts and Social
Studies
Detroit Public Schools
Detroit, Michigan

Edna Whitfield
Former Social Studies Supervisor
St. Louis Public Schools
St. Louis, Missouri

Marilyn Nebenzahl
Social Studies Consultant
San Francisco, California

Karen Wiggins
Director of Social Studies
Richardson Independent School District
Richardson, Texas

Check the Maps•Globes•Graphs Website to find more fun geography activities at home.

Go to www.HarcourtAchieve.com/mggwelcome.html

⟨⟨Harcourt Achieve

Rigby • Steck-Vaughn

www.HarcourtAchieve.com
1.800.531.5015

Acknowledgments

Cartography

Land Registration and Information Service
    Amherst, Nova Scotia, Canada
Gary J. Robinson
MapQuest.com, Inc.
R.R. Donnelley and Sons Company
XNR Productions Inc., Madison, Wisconsin

Photography Credits

COVER (globe, clouds): © PhotoDisc; p. 4 Rusty Kaim; p. 5 (both) © PhotoDisc; p. 6 (top) Rusty Kaim; p. 6 (bottom) © PhotoDisc; p. 7 (top) Park Street; p. 7 (bottom) © PhotoDisc

Illustration Credits

Dennis Harms pp. 50, 51, 55, 56; Michael Krone p. 15; Holly Cooper pp. 23, 65, 66, 67, 68, 69, 70, 71; Rusty Kaim p. 4; Roberta Marco p. 68

ISBN 0-7398-9103-0

© 2004 Harcourt Achieve Inc.

14 15 16 17 18 19 20   1678   18 17 16 15 14 13
4500439688

Contents

Geography Themes

In *Maps•Globes•Graphs* you will learn about ways to study **geography**. Geography is all about Earth and how people live and work on Earth. There are five main ideas people use to study geography.

The Five Themes of Geography
- **Location**
- **Place**
- **Human/Environment Interaction**
- **Movement**
- **Regions**

Location

Location tells where something can be found. You can tell the location of something by naming what it is near or what is around it. You also can tell the location by using an address, or numbers and a street name.

 Kareem lives in this house. Tell the location of his house.

_____

_____

Place

Place tells what a location is like. Each place has **physical features**, or things from nature. These include bodies of water, landforms, weather, plants, and animals. Each place also has **human features**, such as houses, roads, bridges, schools, farms, and factories. People make these.

These pictures show two places. One picture shows the city of St. Louis. The other picture shows Yosemite National Park.

 Name a human feature of St. Louis.

_____

 Name a physical feature of Yosemite National Park.

_____

Human/Environment Interaction

Human/Environment Interaction explains how people live in their environment. **Environment** is the land, water, and air around you. It is the plant and animal life, too. How people make a living often depends on their environment. For example, people who live near the sea might fish for a living.

 How might living on the plains be different from living in the mountains?

_____

_____

_____

Human/Environment Interaction also explains how people change the environment to meet their needs and wants. People might change a field into a parking lot.

 How have people changed the environment in this picture?

_____

_____

Movement

Movement describes how people, goods, information, and ideas get from place to place. People move from place to place in cars and airplanes. How do goods move from place to place?

 How are goods moving in this picture?

_____

Information and ideas move from place to place in newspapers. Information and ideas move in other ways, too.

 How are information and ideas moving in this picture?

Regions

Regions are areas that have something in common. A region may share physical or human features. Regions can be described by such things as climate, plant life, or government. Regions can be as large as your state and as small as your community.

 What feature describes the region in this picture?

Directions and Map Keys

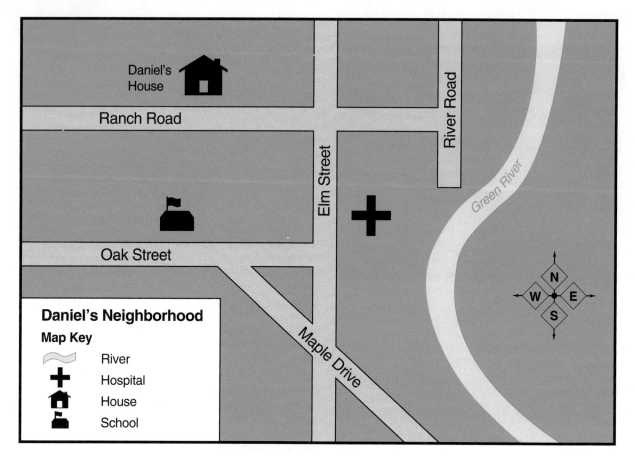

A **map** is a drawing of a real place. A map shows the place from above.

The map above shows Daniel's neighborhood. Use the map to find Daniel's house. What other things does the map show?

Follow these steps to begin reading a map.

MAP ATTACK!

- **Read the title of the map.** The title tells you what the map is about. What is the title of the map on this page?
- **Read the map key.** The map key tells you what each map **symbol** stands for. Match each symbol in the key to a symbol on the map.
- **Read the compass rose.** The compass rose tells you the directions on the map. Find places on the map that are north, south, east, and west of the hospital.

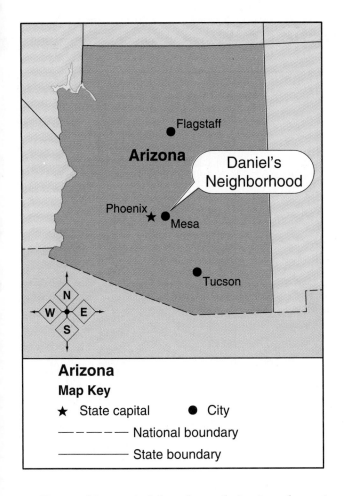

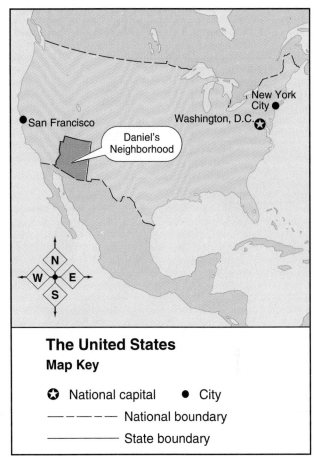

Daniel's neighborhood is in the city of Mesa. Mesa is in the state of Arizona. The map on the left shows the state of Arizona. Find Daniel's city on the map.

Arizona is in a country, the United States. The map on the right shows the United States. Find Daniel's state, Arizona.

You can see that Daniel lives in a neighborhood, a city, a state, and a country all at the same time.

Answer these questions about the map of Arizona. Use the map key and the compass rose.

► Is Mesa east or west of Phoenix?
► Is the state capital north or south of Flagstaff?

Answer these questions about the map of the United States. Use the map key and the compass rose.

► Is New York City north or south of Washington, D.C.?
► Is Arizona east or west of the national capital?

Using Symbols and Directions

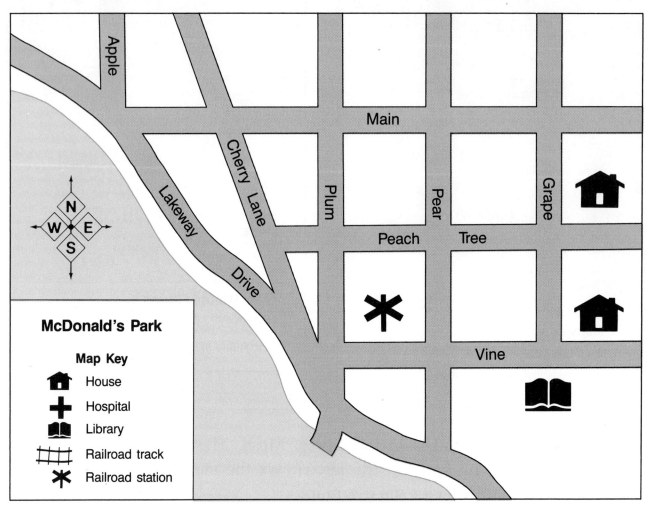

MAP ATTACK!

- **Read the title.** Write it here. _____.
- **Read the map key.** Check (✔) each symbol after you read its meaning. Check (✔) a matching symbol on the map.
- **Read the compass rose.** Circle the north arrow.

Finish the map by adding these symbols.

1. Draw a hospital north of Main between Plum and Pear.
2. Draw a house south of Peach Tree between Pear and Grape.
3. Draw a house east of Apple and north of Main.
4. Draw a railroad track down Plum , from north to south.
5. Draw a house west of Cherry Lane and south of Main.

Using Intermediate Directions

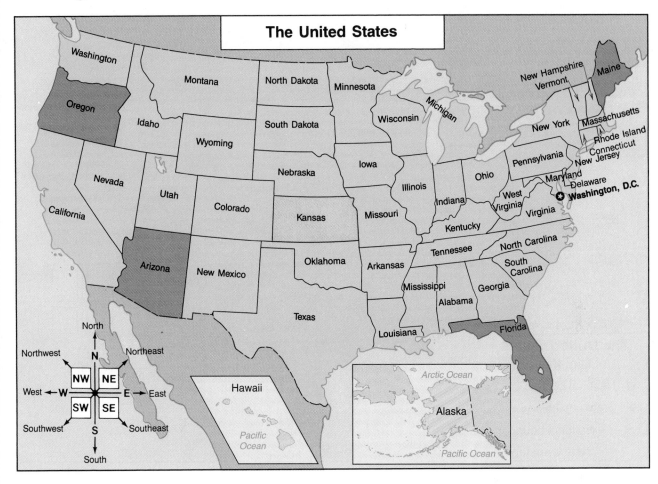

Northeast, southeast, southwest, and northwest are **intermediate directions**. They are also labeled NE, SE, SW, and NW.

1. Which direction is between north and west? _____

2. Which direction is between south and east? _____

3. Northeast is between _____ and _____ .

4. Southwest is between _____ and _____ .

5. To drive from Kansas to Oregon, you go _____ .

6. To drive from Kansas to Florida, you go _____ .

7. To drive from Kansas to Arizona, you go _____ .

8. To drive from Kansas to Maine, you go _____ .

Using Symbols and Intermediate Directions

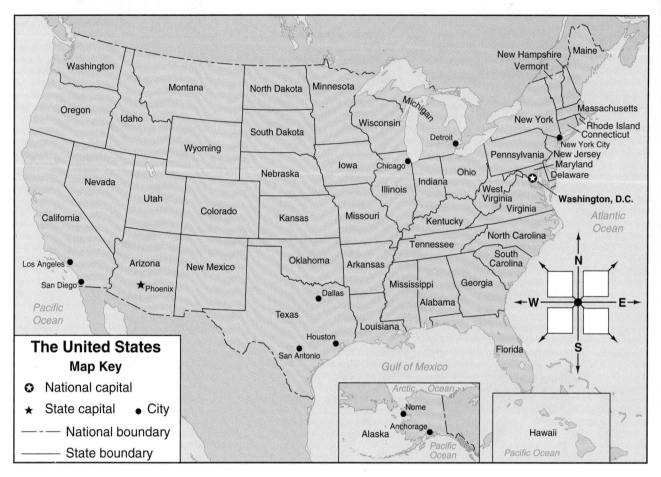

The United States
Map Key
- ✪ National capital
- ★ State capital   • City
- — ·· — National boundary
- ——— State boundary

MAP ATTACK!

Follow the steps on page 8 to begin reading this map.

1. Label the intermediate directions with NE, SE, SW, and NW. Use the compass rose to find these directions.

2. To drive from Arizona to Colorado, you go _____.

3. To drive from New York to Texas, you go _____.

4. Florida is in the _____ part of the United States.

5. New Mexico is in the _____ part of the United States.

6. To drive from San Diego to Los Angeles, you go _____.

7. Chicago is in the _____ part of Illinois.

8. To drive from Nome to Anchorage, you go _____.

Skill Check

 **Test Practice**

Word Check   **map key**   **intermediate directions**
                        title   **compass rose**

Write the word that makes each sentence true.

1. The _____ _____ helps you find directions.

2. The letters NE, SE, SW, and NW stand for

   _____ _____ .

3. The name of a map is its _____ .

4. The _____ _____ explains the symbols
   on a map.

Map Reading Check

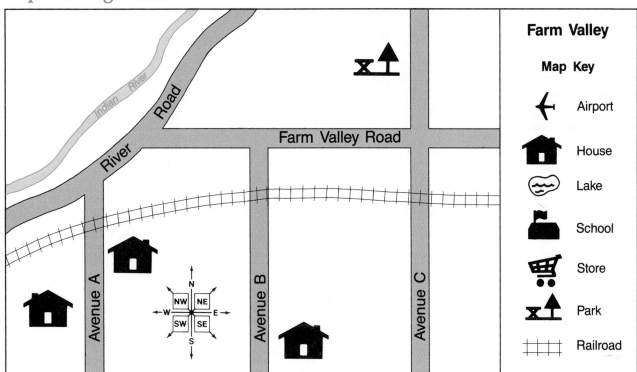

Finish the map of Farm Valley.

1. Draw an airport northwest of Indian River.

2. Draw a lake west of the park.

3. Draw a school south of the railroad near Avenue C.

Distance and Scale

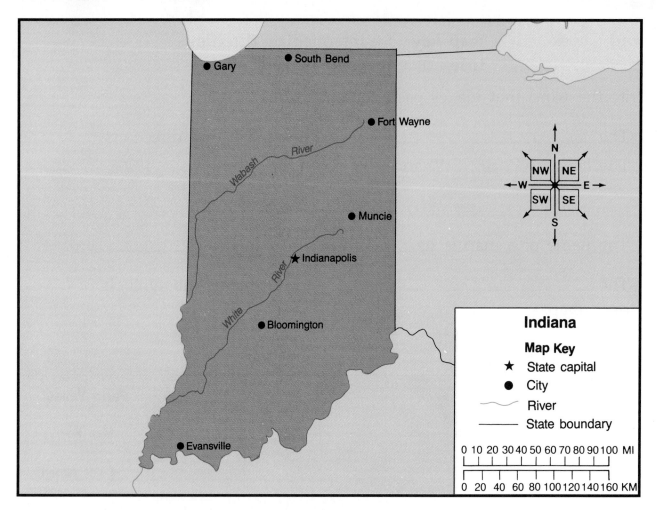

Maps show big places on small pieces of paper. Find Gary and South Bend on the map. Gary is about sixty miles from South Bend. On this map, Gary is about an inch from South Bend.

You can find **distance** on a map by reading a map scale. A **map scale** tells you how many miles in the real world equal an inch on the map.

Some map scales look like this:

```
0                    100   MI
|                      |
0                    160   KM
```

Look at the marks and numbers along the top. They stand for distance in miles. Look at the marks and numbers along the bottom. They stand for distance in kilometers. **Miles** and **kilometers** are two ways of measuring distance.

▶ Find the map scale on the Indiana map.
▶ What letters stand for miles?
▶ What letters stand for kilometers?

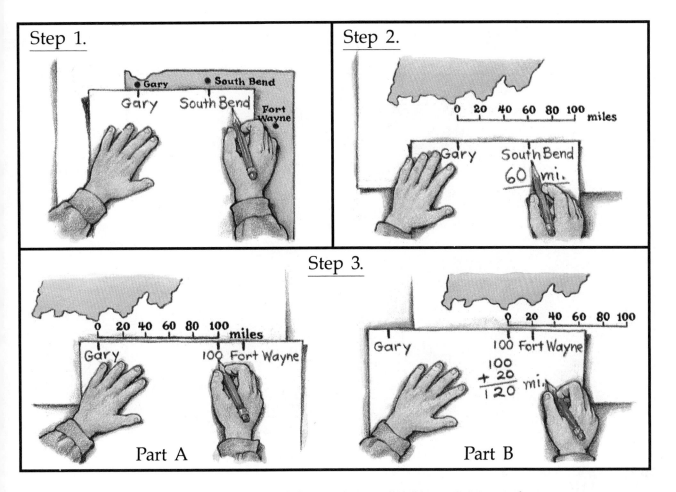

Step 1.

Step 2.

Step 3.

Part A

Part B

Suppose you want to find the distance between Gary and South Bend. Here's how to use the map scale:

Step 1. Lay the edge of a piece of paper in a straight line from Gary to South Bend. Mark your paper below each city.

Step 2. Lay the edge of your paper along the scale. Your left-hand mark should be below "0". Read the scale numbers nearest your right-hand mark. The numbers tell you that Gary and South Bend are about 60 miles apart.

Step 3. What if the distance between two cities is greater than the scale? Lay your paper on the scale and mark your paper below the highest number on the scale. Then move your paper so that your new mark is below "0". Read the scale number nearest your right-hand mark. Add that number to the highest number on the scale. The sum is your distance.

► Can you find the distance between Fort Wayne and South Bend?

Figuring Distances on a Map

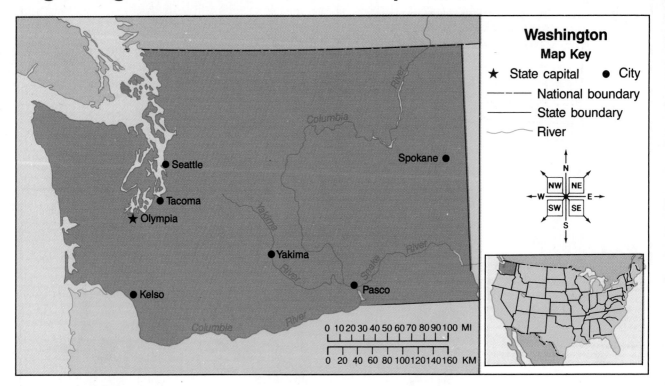

MAP ATTACK!

● The title of the map is _____.

● The state capital is _____.

● The scale goes up to _____ miles.

Use the edge of a paper and the scale to figure these distances. If your marks fall between the scale marks, try to estimate the distance. Write the distance in miles.

1. From Kelso to Seattle is about _____ miles.

2. From Seattle to Olympia is about _____ miles.

3. From Yakima to Spokane is about _____ miles.

4. From Tacoma to Spokane is about _____ miles.

5. From Olympia to Yakima is about _____ miles.

Figuring Distances

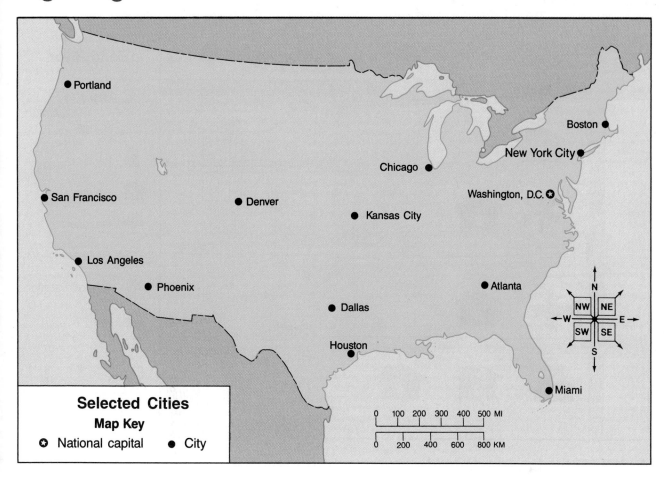

MAP ATTACK!

Follow the steps on page 8 to begin reading this map.

Use the map scale and the edge of a paper to find these distances.

1. From Phoenix to Dallas is about _____ miles.

2. From Portland to Chicago is about _____ miles.

3. From Boston to Kansas City is about _____ miles.

4. From Atlanta to Houston is about _____ miles.

5. From New York City to Miami is about _____ miles.

6. From Los Angeles to Chicago is about _____ miles.

7. From San Francisco to Denver is about _____ miles.

Reading a Map

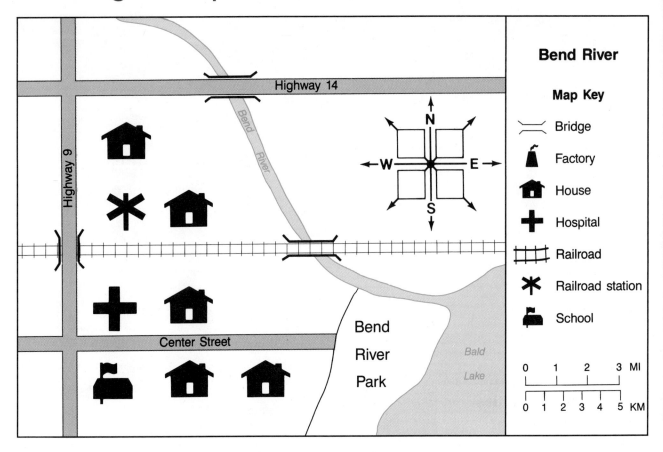

1. Label the intermediate directions on the compass rose.

2. Draw a factory northeast of the railroad station near the houses.

3. The hospital is at the corner of _____ and

   _____ .

Name the direction that finishes the sentence.

4. The railroad station is _____ of the river.

5. The Bend River runs _____ toward the lake.

6. The school is _____ of the hospital.

Use the map scale and the edge of a piece of paper to find these distances.

7. The railroad bridge over Bend River is about _____ miles long.

8. From Highway 14 to Center Street is about _____ miles.

Skill Check

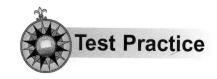

Word Check   **map scale** **distance**
       miles   **kilometers**

Use each word to finish a sentence. Use one word twice.

1. _____ is how far apart places are.

2. A _____ is used to figure distances on a map.

3. Kilometers and miles measure _____ on Earth.

4. The letters **KM** stand for _____ .

5. The letters **MI** stand for _____ .

Map Scale Check

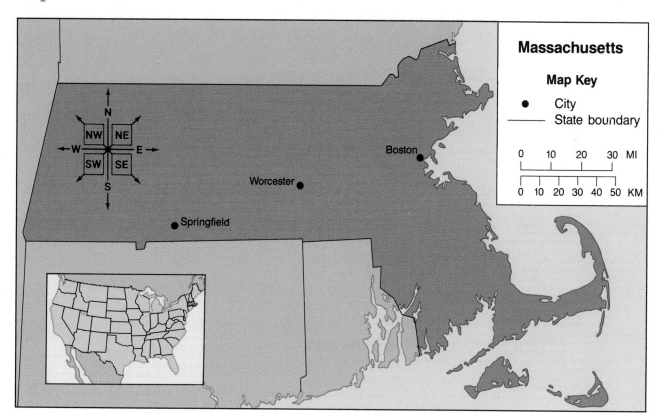

Use the scale and a piece of paper to find these distances.

1. Springfield is about _____ miles from Worcester.

2. Boston is about _____ miles from Springfield.

Place describes a location. Are there hills there? What kinds of buildings are there? The physical and human features of each place make it special.

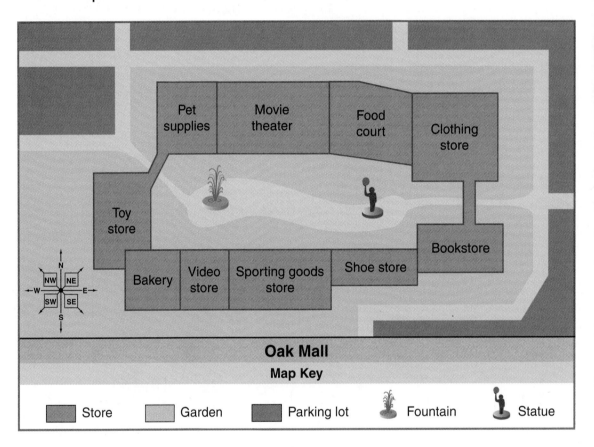

Oak Mall

Map Key

Store　　Garden　　Parking lot　　Fountain　　Statue

1. What store is north of the bookstore?

_____

2. List three features of Oak Mall.

_____

_____

3. Find the toy store on the map. Circle it. Mark **P** on it if it is a physical feature. Mark **H** if it is a human feature.

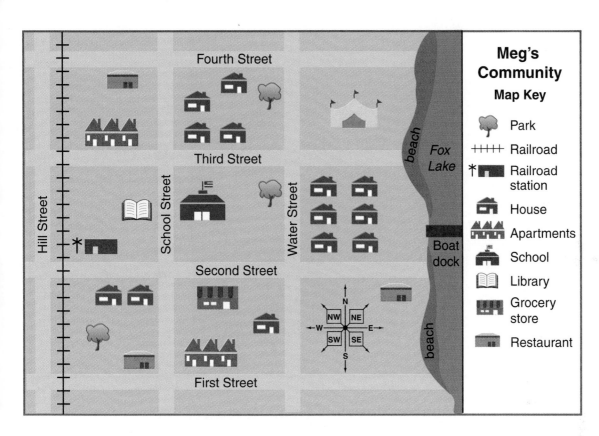

Meg's Community
Map Key

- 🌳 Park
- +++++ Railroad
- ✝🏢 Railroad station
- 🏠 House
- 🏘 Apartments
- 🏫 School
- 📖 Library
- 🏪 Grocery store
- 🏛 Restaurant

Fourth Street

Third Street

Second Street

First Street

Hill Street

School Street

Water Street

Fox Lake

beach

Boat dock

beach

N / NW / NE / W / E / SW / SE / S

4. Find the fairgrounds on the map above. They are west of Fox Lake. Label them on the map. Mark **P** if they are a physical feature. Mark **H** if they are a human feature.

5. Name a physical feature of Meg's community. Mark it with **P** on the map.

_____

6. What features in Meg's community make it different from your community?

_____

_____

_____

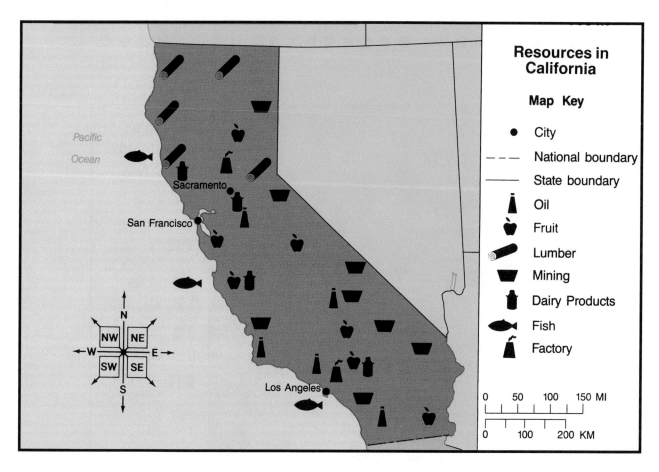

This map shows the resources in California. **Resources** are things people can use. The map also shows the areas where those resources are found. Find the factory symbols on the map. A **factory** is a place where resources are made into other things.

Use your map attack skills to begin reading this map.

MAP ATTACK!

- **Read the title.** The title tells you the purpose of the map and what the map shows.
- **Study the key.** Read the meanings of the symbols. Find each symbol on the map. Which resources are near cities? Which are on land? Which are in water?
- **Read the compass rose.** Find north on the map. Which resources are in the north? in the south? in the east? in the west? in the center?

The resources you see on the map on page 22 can be grouped in different ways. Grouping them makes them easier to study and remember. Some of the resources come from animals. Some come from plants. Others are minerals found in the earth. This table shows California's resources listed in the three groups.

California's Resources		
Animal Resources	Plant Resources	Mineral Resources
dairy products	fruit	mining
fish	lumber	oil

Resources can also be grouped by place. Which symbols are mainly in the north? in the south? in the east? in the west? This table shows California's resources by place.

California's Resources by Place	
Resources mainly in the east:	mining ▬ fruit 🍎
Resources mainly in the west:	fishing 🐟 dairy products 🍶
Resources mainly in the north:	lumber 🪵
Resources mainly in the south:	oil ▮

Reading a Resource Map

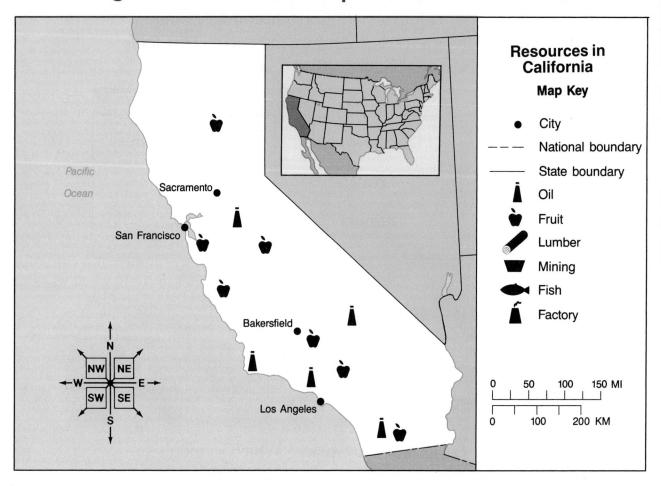

Follow the four steps to begin reading this map.

MAP ATTACK!

- **Read the title.** Write it here. _____
- **Read the map key.** Check (✔) each symbol after you read its meaning. Check (✔) a matching symbol on the map.
- **Read the compass rose.** Circle the north arrow.
- **Read the map scale.** Circle the names of the two ways distance is measured on the map scale.

1. Draw four factory symbols, one each near San Francisco, Los Angeles, Bakersfield, and Sacramento.

2. Draw three mining symbols along California's eastern boundary.

3. Draw three fishing symbols off the western coastline.

4. Draw three lumber symbols near the northern boundary.

Reading a Resource Map

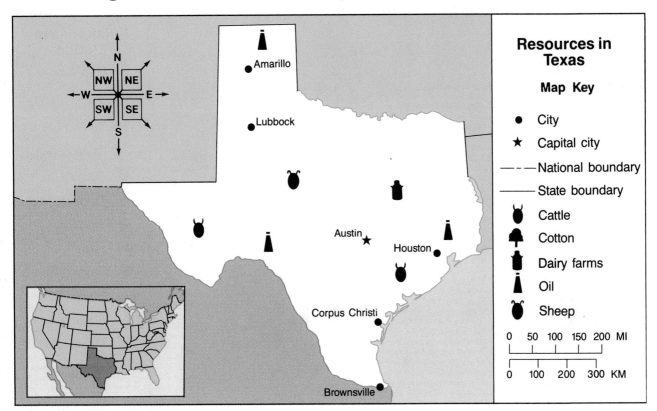

Resources in Texas

Map Key

- City
★ Capital city
- - - National boundary
——— State boundary
Cattle
Cotton
Dairy farms
Oil
Sheep

0   50   100   150   200   MI

0   100   200   300   KM

MAP ATTACK!

- The title of the map is _____ .

- The state capital is _____ .

- The distance from Austin to Houston is _____ miles.

1. Draw a cotton symbol southwest of Corpus Christi.

2. Draw one cotton symbol north of Austin, one north of Lubbock, and one north of Brownsville.

3. Draw two oil symbols, one near Lubbock and one near Houston.

4. Draw two cattle symbols, one northwest of Amarillo, and one northwest of Austin.

5. Circle the resource that is produced in more places.

cotton or dairy   sheep or cattle   oil or cotton

Reading a Resource Map

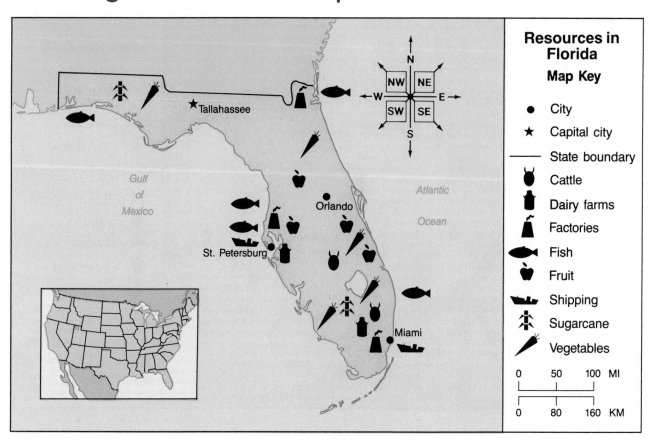

1. What does the map show? (What is the title?)

   _____

2. Circle Florida on the small U.S. map. Is Florida in the northern

   or southern U.S.? _____

Use the map scale and the edge of a piece of paper to find these distances.

3. From St. Petersburg to Orlando is about _____ miles.

4. From St. Petersburg to Miami is about _____ miles.

5. Which cities are on the coast?

   _____   _____

6. Name three of the most important resources in Florida.

   _____ _____ _____

Skill Check

Word Check   **factory**   **resource**

Write the word that makes each sentence true.

1. A _____ is something that people use.

2. Resources are made into other things at a _____.

Resource Map Check

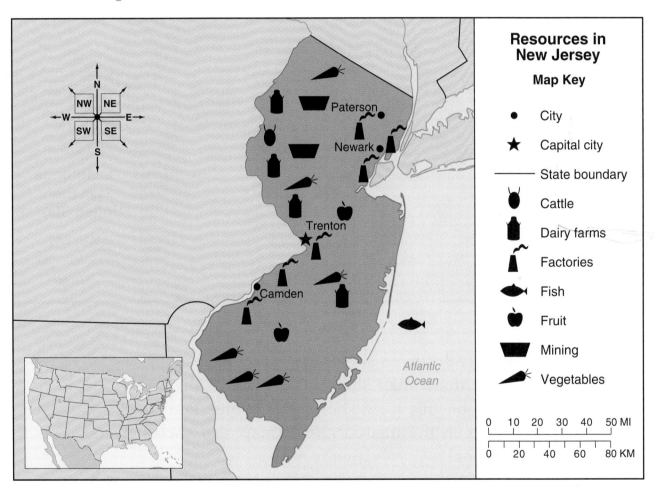

1. Cattle and dairy farms are mainly in the _____ part of New Jersey.

2. The main resource in the south is _____.

3. Circle the resource that is produced in more places.

   cattle or dairy   fruit or fish   mining or vegetables

4. What are located near the cities? _____

Landform Maps

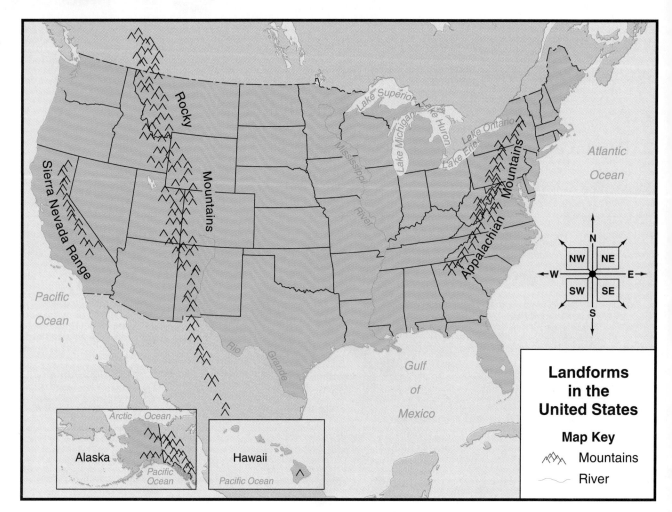

Map A

The shape of the land can be shown on maps in many different ways. A **landform map** shows the shape of the land.

The landform map on this page shows mountains. Find the symbol for mountains in the map key. This map also shows rivers, large lakes, and oceans.

The landform map on the next page shows areas of landforms. The areas are different colors. The highest landform is the darkest color. Which landform is highest? The lowest landform is the lightest color. These are **plains**, or flat lands.

Find the areas of plateaus. A **plateau** is high, flat land.

Find the Gulf of Mexico. A **gulf** is a large body of water that cuts deep into the land.

Land next to the ocean is called the **coast**. What states have some coast?

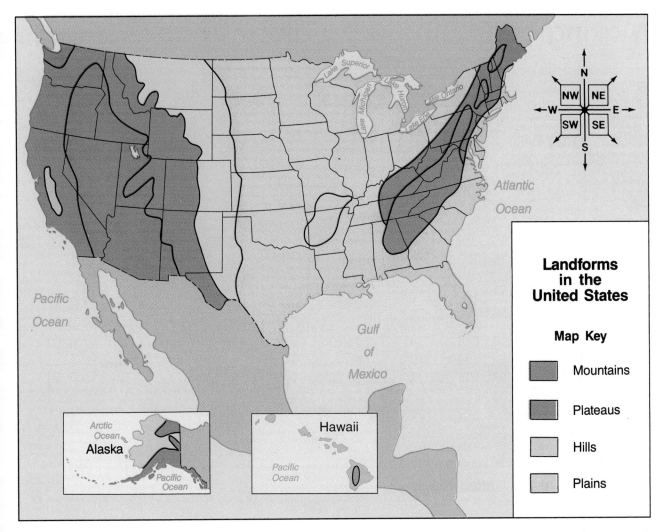

Map B

Compare Map A and Map B.

1. What landforms are only on Map B? _____

   _____

2. What bodies of water are only on Map A? _____

3. Are there more mountains in the eastern or the western

   United States? _____

4. Where are most of the plains? _____

5. What landform is on the west coast? _____

6. Circle the label for a gulf on both maps.

Making and Using a Landform Map

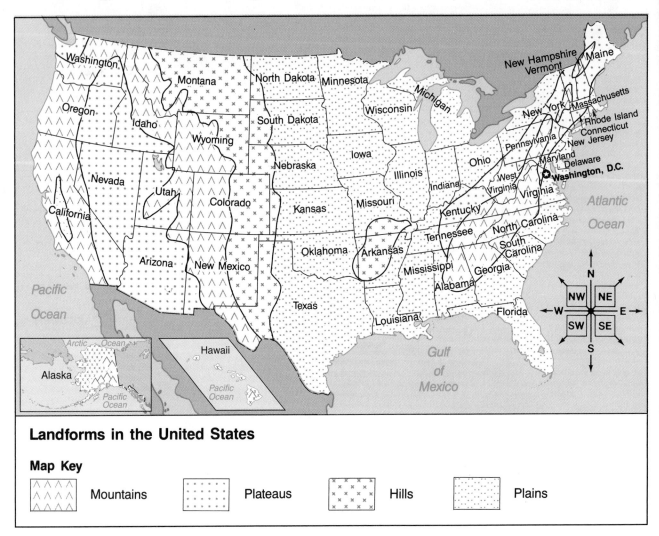

Landforms in the United States

Map Key

Mountains | Plateaus | Hills | Plains

MAP ATTACK!

- **Read the title.** Write it here. _____
- **Read the compass rose.** Circle the intermediate direction arrows.

1. Color the map key. Use colored pens or pencils. Choose four colors for the landform areas.

2. Color the map to match the key.

3. Which landform(s) does your state have? _____

_____

Reading a Landform Map

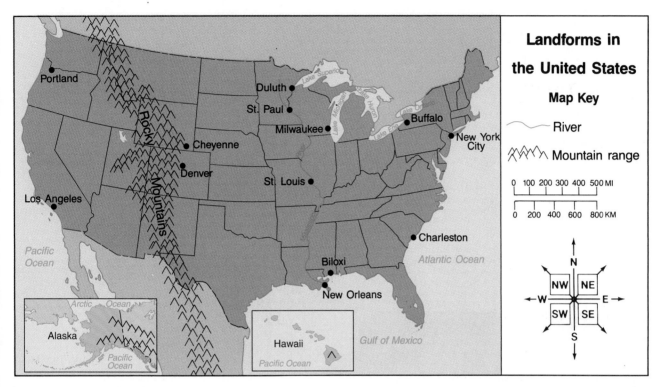

Landforms in the United States

Map Key

~~~ River

ⱯⱯⱯ Mountain range

0 100 200 300 400 500 MI

0   200 400 600 800 KM

MAP ATTACK!

● The title of the map is _____ .

● From New York City to Buffalo is about _____ miles.

1. Name a city on the west coast. _____

2. Name a city on the east coast. _____

3. Name a city on the Gulf of Mexico coast. _____

4. Name two cities on the edge of the Great Lakes.

_____   _____

5. Name two cities on the eastern edge of the Rocky Mountains.

_____   _____

6. Name two cities on the Mississippi River.

_____   _____

Making and Using a Landform Map

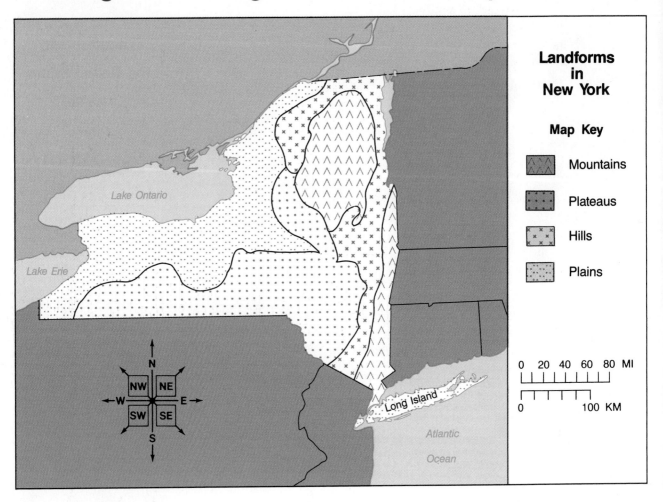

MAP ATTACK!

Follow the steps on page 24 to begin reading this map.

1. Color the landform areas to match the key.
   Use colored pencils or pens.

2. New York's plains are mostly in the _____ .

3. New York's mountains are mostly in the _____ .

4. What lakes form part of New York's western boundary?

   _____   _____

5. Long Island is about _____ miles long.

6. Lake Ontario is about _____ miles long (east to west).

Skill Check

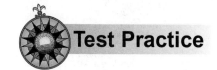
Word Check   plateau   gulf
                   coast   landform map

Write the word that makes each sentence true.

1. A _____ is high, flat land.

2. A _____ is a large body of water that cuts deep into the land.

3. A _____ is land next to the ocean.

Landform Map Check

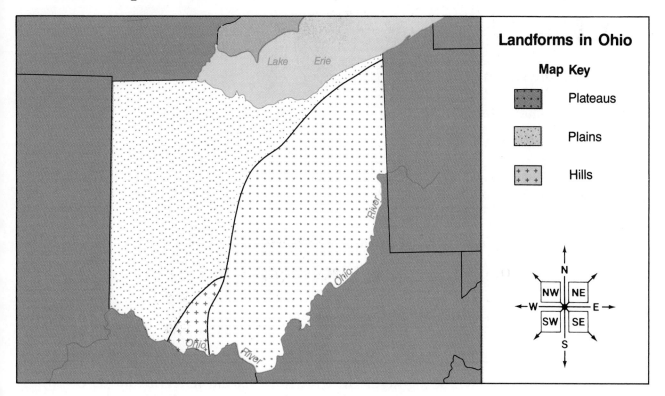

1. Color the landform areas to match the key.

2. Ohio's plains are mostly in which direction? _____

   Ohio's plateaus are mostly in the _____ .

3. What lake forms part of Ohio's northern boundary? _____

4. What river forms Ohio's southern boundary? _____

Geography Themes Up Close

Regions are areas that share the same feature. The map below shows plant regions in the United States.

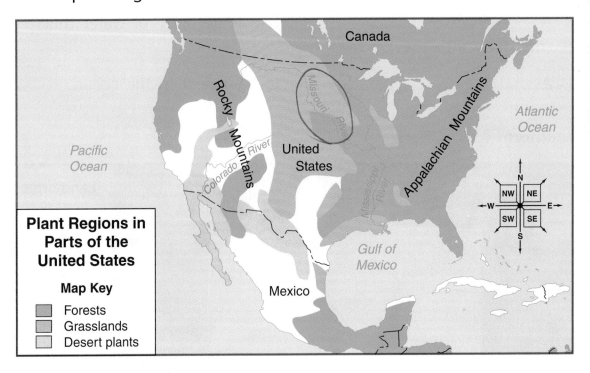

Canada

Rocky Mountains

Missouri River

Colorado River

United States

Appalachian Mountains

Atlantic Ocean

Pacific Ocean

Mississippi River

N
NW   NE
W   E
SW   SE
S

Gulf of Mexico

Mexico

Plant Regions in Parts of the United States

Map Key

Forests
Grasslands
Desert plants

1. What three plant regions are shown on this map?

   This map shows forests, Grasslands and desertplants

2. Which plant region is largest?

   The Forest one is biggest

3. Find the Missouri River on the map. Circle it. What kinds of plants mostly grow along the Missouri River?

   Forests

4. What kinds of plants grow along the border of the United States and Mexico?

   desert plants

The map shows Desmond Park—one of ten community parks in Elm City. All the parks in Elm City have the same features.

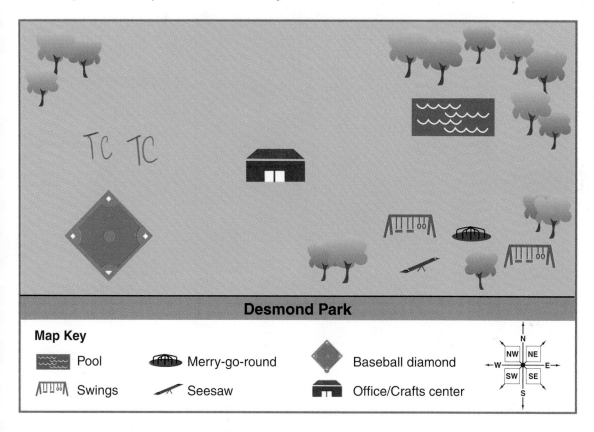

Desmond Park

Map Key

Pool	Merry-go-round	Baseball diamond
Swings	Seesaw	Office/Crafts center

5. There are tennis courts north of the baseball diamond. Mark **TC** on the map for the tennis courts.

6. What direction is the pool from the baseball diamond?

   north east

7. What activity is held in the Desmond Park office building?

   Crafts

8. Why do you think the parks in Elm City form a region?

   They are the same

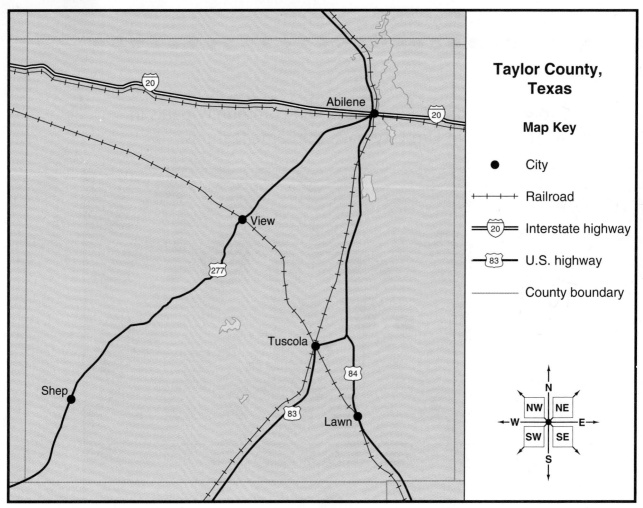

A **route** is a way of getting from one place to another. There are many different kinds of routes. Roads and railroads are routes. What are some other kinds of routes?

The map on this page shows routes. What different kinds of routes does the map show?

▶ Study the map key. What does each symbol stand for?

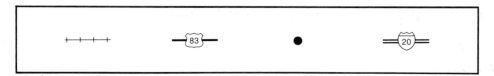

▶ Which city has the most routes going through it?
▶ Which route goes through Shep?
▶ Which routes go through Tuscola?
▶ Which route runs along Interstate highway 20?

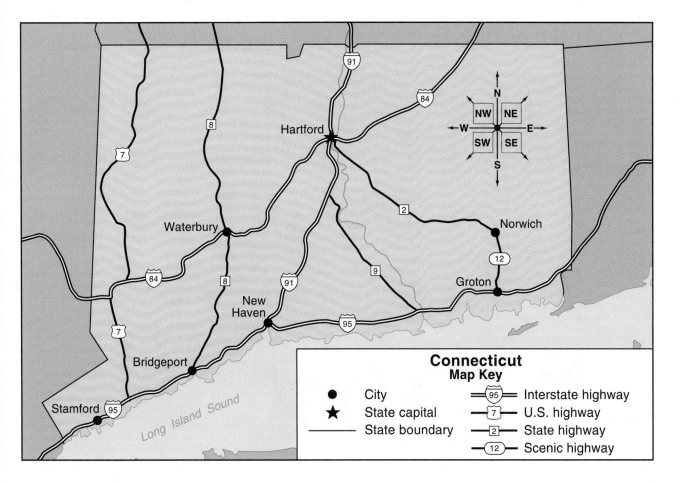

Most route maps show roads. This is because most routes are roads. Look at the map above. It shows main roads in Connecticut. Main roads are called **highways**.

Not all highways are the same. How many different kinds of highways do you see on the map? The map key tells you how the different kinds of highways are marked on the map.

► Study the map key. Find the symbol for a state highway. Find a state highway on the map.

► Find the symbol for a scenic highway. Find a scenic highway on the map.

► What kind of highway goes from Waterbury to Hartford?

► What kind of highway goes from Hartford to Norwich?

► What kind of highway goes along the water?

► What two cities does the scenic highway go through?

► What kind of highway is Highway 7?

► Which highway would you take from Hartford to New Haven?

Reading a Route Map

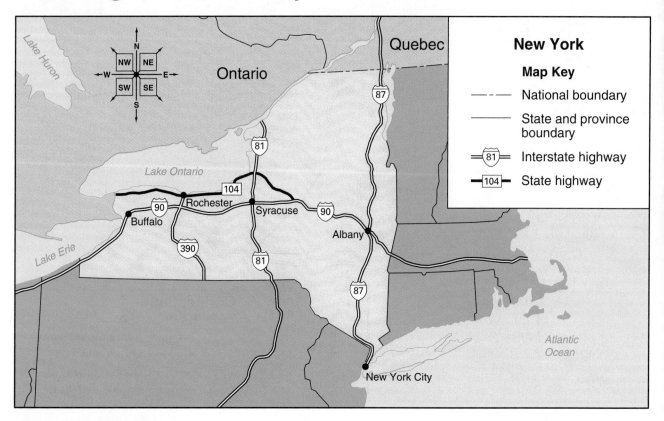

MAP ATTACK!

- **Read the title.** Write it here. _____
- **Read the key.** There are two types of highways. An **interstate highway** goes through more than one state. A **state highway** does not.
- **Read the compass rose.** Circle the arrow that points north.

1. How many interstate highways are in New York? _____

2. What highway runs along the coast of Lake Ontario? _____

3. What cities are along Highway 90? _____

   _____   _____

4. What highway goes south from Syracuse? _____

5. What highway would take you into Quebec, Canada? _____

Reading a Route Map

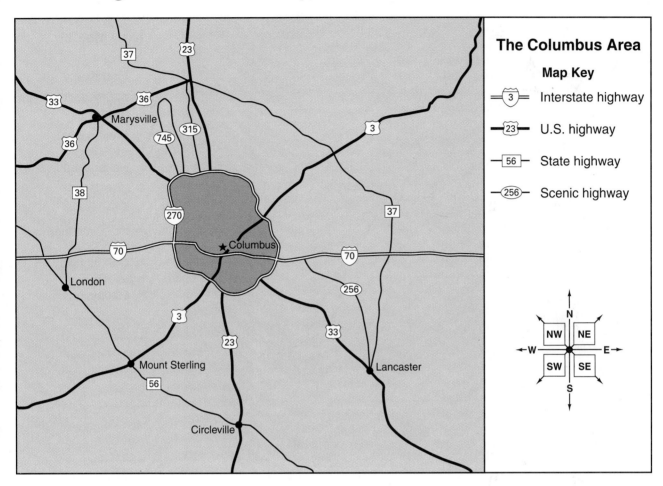

1. What highway goes around Columbus? _____

2. What highways would take you into downtown Columbus?

   _____   _____

3. Scenic Highway 256 connects Interstate 70 with what city?

   _____

4. Which scenic highway begins and ends at Interstate 270? _____

5. If you travelled from Circleville to Marysville on Highways 56 and 38, what cities would you drive through?

   _____   _____

6. What highways would you take from Lancaster to Marysville

   without going to Columbus? _____   _____

Reading a Route and Landform Map

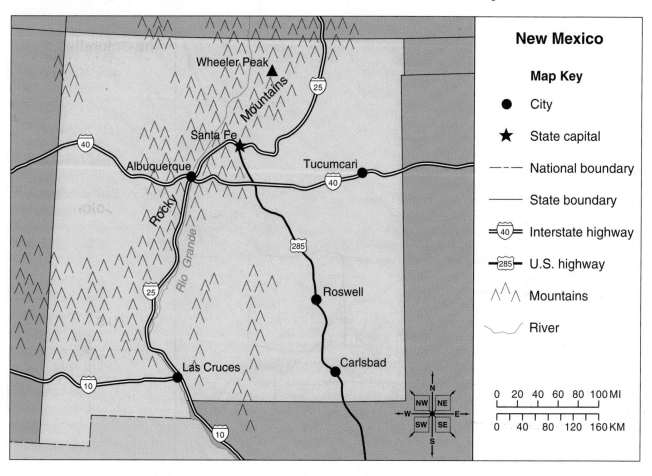

MAP ATTACK!

Follow the steps on page 38 to begin reading this map.

1. What three interstate highways go through New Mexico?

   40, 25, 10

2. Circle the city that is in the mountains.

   (Santa Fe)   Roswell   Carlsbad

3. What kind of highway is Highway 285? _U.S. Highway_

4. To drive from Roswell to Carlsbad, which direction should

   you go? _South_ About how far is it? _7 mi_

5. What two cities are on the Rio Grande?

   _A_

Skill Check

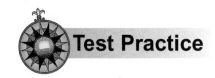

Word Check   **route**

Use <u>route</u> in a sentence that shows its meaning.

_____

Route Map Check

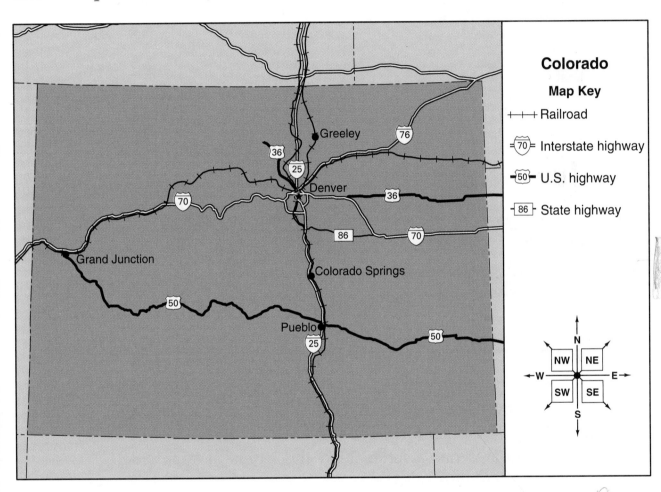

Colorado

Map Key

+—+—+ Railroad

=⟨70⟩= Interstate highway

–⟨50⟩– U.S. highway

–|86|– State highway

1. What routes can you take between Greeley and Grand Junction?

    _Railroad Hwy 70, 25._

2. Which city has the most routes leading to it? _Denver_

3. Which interstate highways lead to Denver? _76, 25, 70_

4. Which U.S. highway leads to Denver? _36_

5. Which state highway leads to Denver? _86_

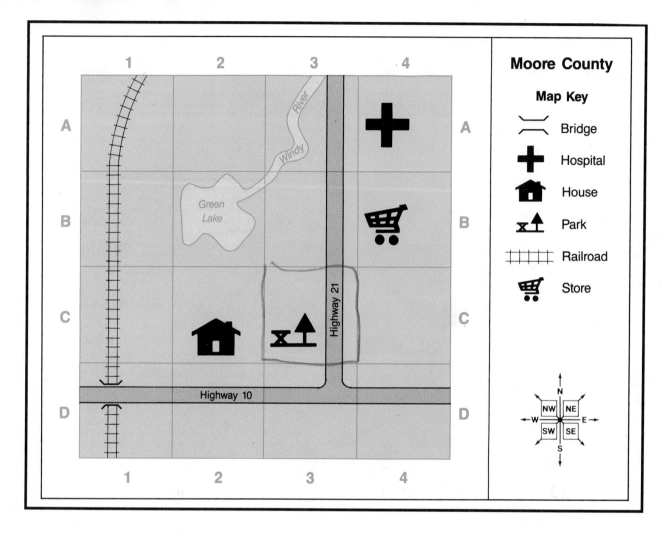

Sometimes you want to say exactly where a place is on a map. You can do this by using a grid. A **grid** is a pattern of lines that cross each other. The lines form squares.

Each row of squares has a letter. Find the letters at each side of the map. What letters are used?

Each column of squares has a number. Find the numbers across the top and the bottom of the map. What numbers are used?

Each square on the map is named with a letter and a number.

Here is how to find square A-2. Put your finger on the letter A. Move your finger across the row. Stop when you come to column 2. This is square A-2.

▶ Can you find square C-3?

▶ In which square is the store?

▶ Which squares does the railroad go through?

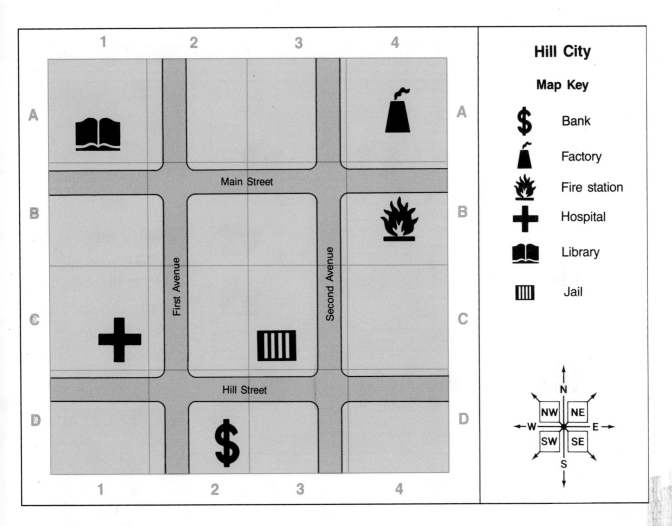

A **map index** is an alphabetical list of places on the map. The index tells in which square you can find each place. Suppose you need to find the hospital. Look under H in the index below. Read the letter and number of the square next to the word <u>hospital</u>.

Now find the hospital on the map. Put your finger on C. Move across that row until you are in column 1. The hospital is in square C-1.

Complete this index by finding the square for each place.

<u>Map Index</u>

| Bank _____ | Fire Station _____ | Jail _____ |
| Factory _____ | Hospital **C-1** | Library _____ |

D-2

Using a Map Grid

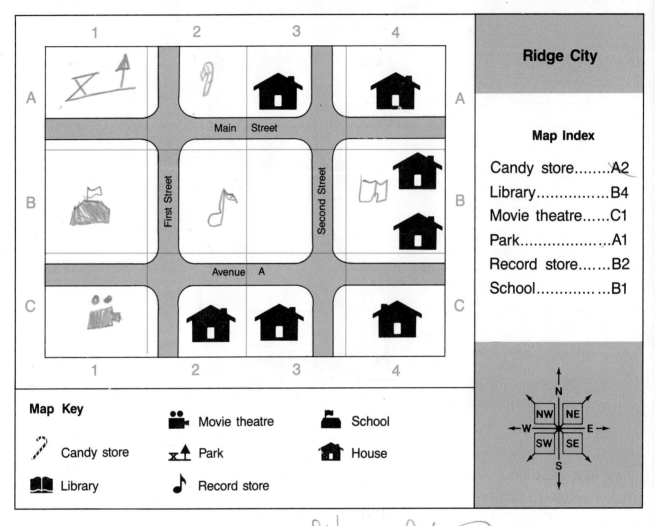

Ridge City

Map Index

Candy store........A2
Library..............B4
Movie theatre......C1
Park.................A1
Record store.......B2
School..............B1

Map Key

🎥 Movie theatre   🏫 School

🍬 Candy store   ⛺ Park   🏠 House

📖 Library   ♪ Record store

1. What city does this map show? _Ridge City_

2. Study the map index.
   Draw the buildings from the index on the map where they belong.

3. What street runs through squares A-1, A-2, A-3, and A-4?
   Main Street

4. What street runs through squares A-3, B-3, and C-3?
   Second Street

5. What building is in square C-3? _House_

6. Which square has the most buildings in it? _4-B_

Using a Map Grid

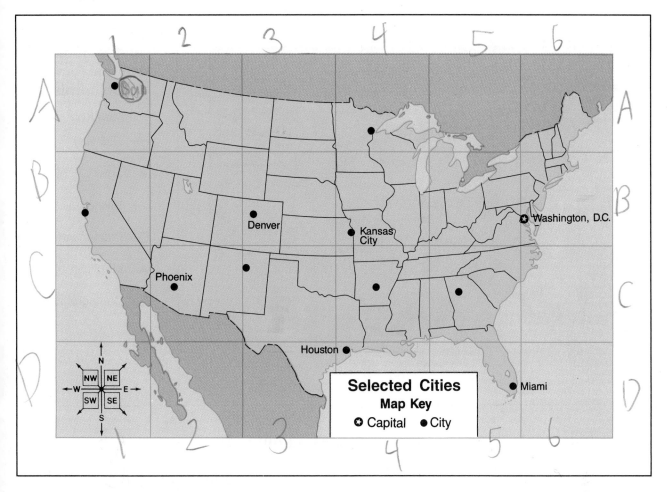

1. Finish the grid. Write the letters A, B, C, and D down each side. Write the numbers 1, 2, 3, 4, 5, and 6 across the top and bottom.

2. In which square is each place?

   Washington, D.C. _B6_   Miami _D5_

   Houston _D3_   Phoenix _C-2_

   Denver _B3_   Kansas City _B4_

3. Find these cities on the map. Label each city.
   San Francisco B-1   Olympia A-1   Little Rock C-4
   Duluth   A-4   Santa Fe C-3   Atlanta   C-5

4. If you drove from Denver to Washington, D.C., what

   squares would you drive in? _B6_ _B5_ _B4_ _B3_

Using a Map Grid

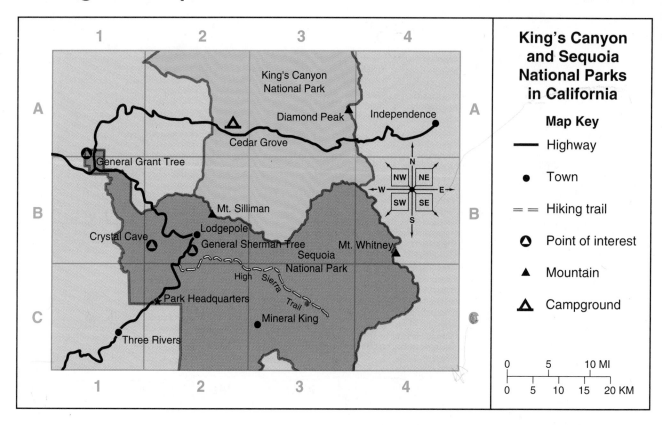

1. The following places are in which grid squares?

   Independence _A4_   Mineral King _C3_   Cedar Grove _A3_ ~~AE~~ 3

   Park Headquarters _C-2_   Mt. Silliman _B2_   Mt. Whitney _B4_

2. High Sierra Trail goes through which squares? _B-2_ _C-2_ _C-3_

3. Complete this table. Use the map scale to find the distance.
   Use the compass rose to find the direction.

	Direction	Miles
▶ from Lodgepole to Diamond Peak	NE	28 miles
▶ from General Sherman Tree to General Grant Tree	NW	18
▶ from Independence to Cedar Grove	NW	28
▶ from Crystal Cave to Park Headquarters	S	8

Skill Check

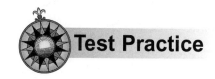
Word Check   **grid**   **index**

Write the word that best completes each sentence.

1. A _____ is a pattern of lines that cross each other.

2. A map _____ is an alphabetical list of places on the map.

Map Check

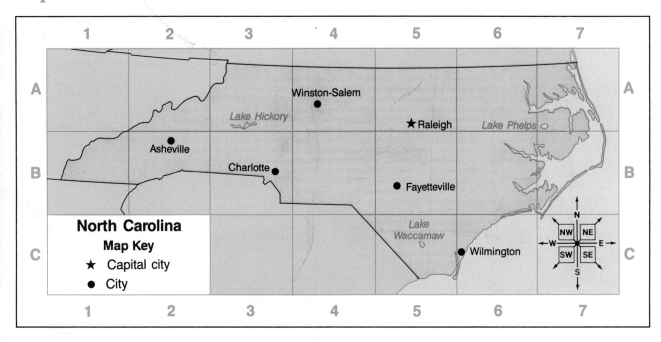

1. Name North Carolina's capital and the letter and number of

   its grid square. _____ _____

2. Complete the map index below.

_____	B-2	Lake Phelps	_____
Charlotte	_____	Lake Waccamaw	_____
Fayetteville	_____	Wilmington	_____
_____	A-3	_____	A-4

Geography Themes Up Close

Movement explains how people, goods, and ideas get from one place to another. Movement also tells how people in a community depend on people in other communities for goods and services.

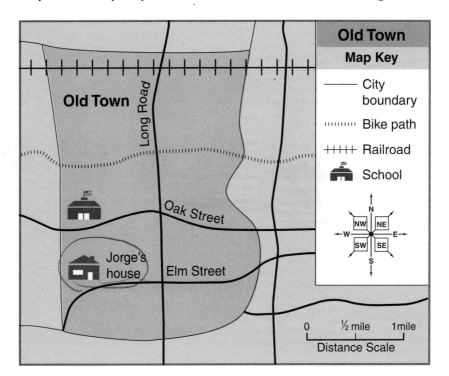

1. The map above shows Old Town where Jorge and his family live. Find Jorge's house on the map and circle it.

2. Name three kinds of transportation routes in Old Town.

   Bike path, Railroad, Streets,

3. What route would Jorge's mother take to drive him to school?

   Elmstreet Longroad oak street

4. Jorge's family likes to ride on the bike path. How far is the bike path from Jorge's house?

   The Path is two miles

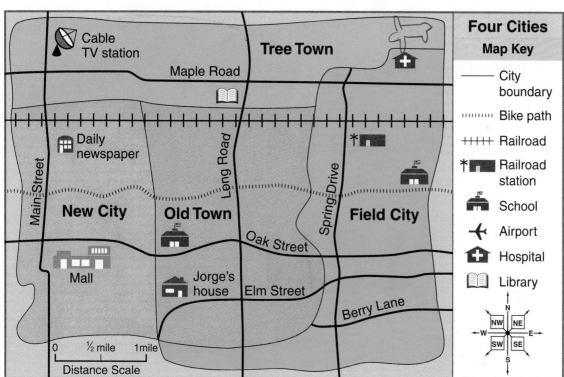

Four Cities

Map Key

——	City boundary
....	Bike path
++++	Railroad
*▮▮	Railroad station
🏫	School
✈	Airport
✚	Hospital
📖	Library

5. Where can Jorge go to shop at stores?

Jorge can go Shopping in the mall

6. Name two ways ideas move in these communities.

Word and Newspaper

7. Where can Jorge and his family go to get on the train?

Field city All

8. The people in the four communities want an airport. Draw a symbol on the map where you would put the airport. Tell why this would be a good place to build an airport.

I think I should put it there because

7 Latitude

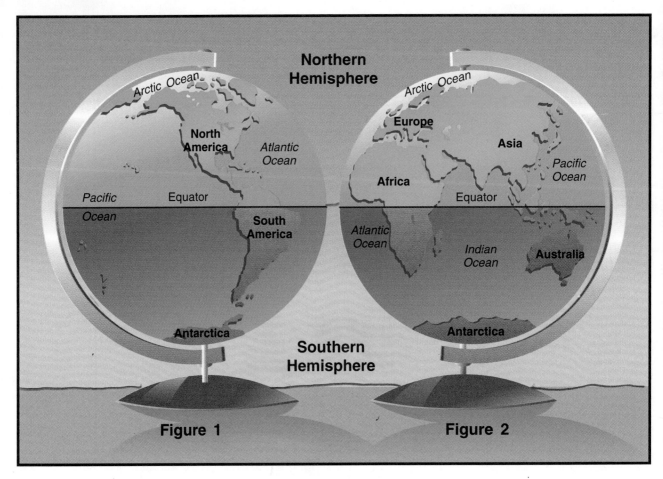

Figure 1   Figure 2

One of the most important lines on the globe is the **Equator**. The Equator is an imaginary line that goes around the middle of Earth. Study Figure 1 and Figure 2. Find the Equator on both sides of the globe.

The Equator divides the globe into two halves. Each half is called a **hemisphere**. Half the globe north of the Equator is the **Northern Hemisphere**. Half the globe south of the Equator is the **Southern Hemisphere**.

► Look at Figure 1.
  Find the land in the Northern Hemisphere. It is colored green.
  Find the land in the Southern Hemisphere. It is colored brown.

► Look at Figure 2.
  One continent is both north and south of the Equator.
  Look for the continent that is both green and brown.
  What is the name of that continent?

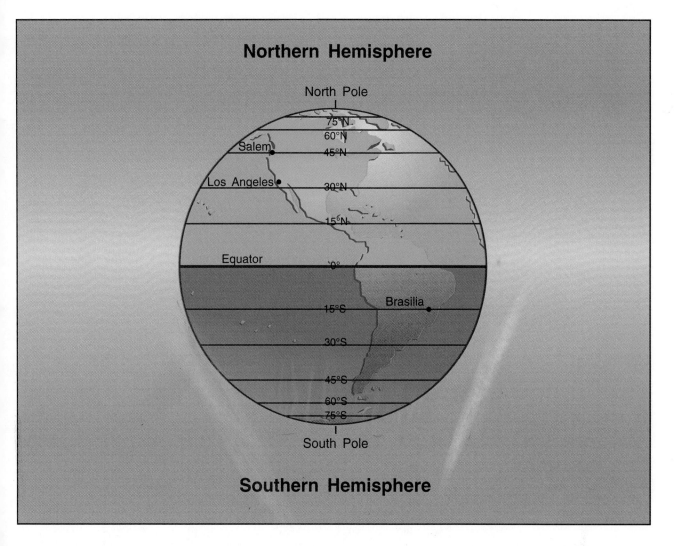

Northern Hemisphere

North Pole
75°N
60°N
45°N
Salem
Los Angeles
30°N
15°N
Equator
0°
15°S
Brasilia
30°S
45°S
60°S
75°S
South Pole

Southern Hemisphere

Find the Equator on the globe above. Now find the lines above and below the Equator. These are called **lines of latitude**. We use lines of latitude to locate places north and south of the Equator.

Lines of latitude are marked by **degrees**. The symbol ° stands for degrees. The Equator is at 0° latitude.

► Look at the Northern Hemisphere.
  Find the 45° North latitude line.
  What city is at 45° North?

► Look at the Southern Hemisphere.
  Find the 15° South latitude line.
  What city is at 15° South?

► Look at the whole globe.
  Find Los Angeles.
  What line of latitude is it near?

Finding Latitude

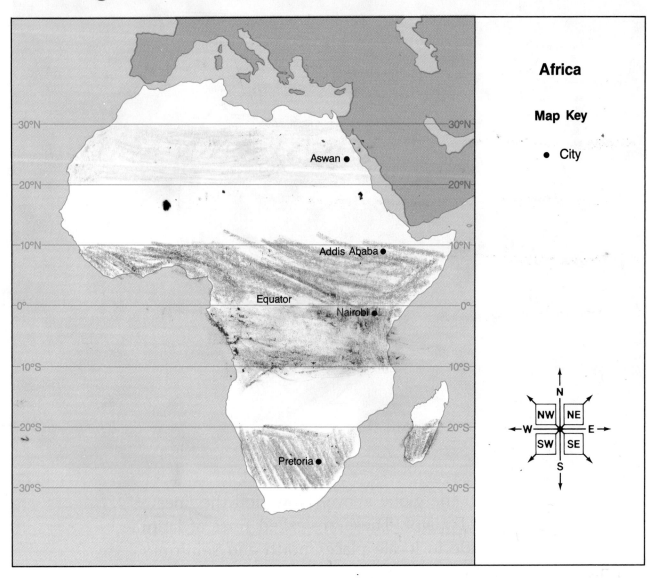

Africa

Map Key

• City

1. Color Africa green between 20°N and 30°N.

   What city lies in that area? __Aswan__

2. Color Africa brown between 0° and 10°N.

   What city lies in that area? __Addis Ababa__

3. Color Africa yellow between 0° and 10°S.

   What city lies in that area? __Nairobi__

4. Color Africa orange between 20°S and 30°S.

   What city lies in that area? __Pretoria__

Finding Latitude

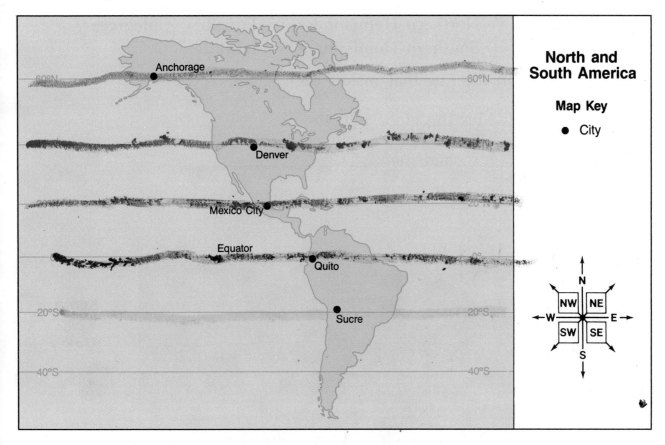

North and South America

Map Key

● City

You can find a place if you know which line of latitude it is on. Every city on this map is on a line of latitude.

1. Find the Equator. Trace it in red.

   What city is on the Equator? _Kito_

2. Find the 20°South line of latitude. Trace it in green.

   What city is at 20°South? _Sucre_

3. Find the 20°North line of latitude. Trace it in purple.

   What city is at 20°North? _Mexico_

4. Find the 40°North line of latitude. Trace it in orange.

   What city is at 40°North? _Denver_

5. Find the 60°North line of latitude. Trace it in blue.

   What city is at 60°North? _Anchorage_

Skill Check

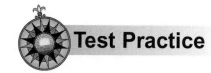

Test Practice

Word Check   **Northern Hemisphere**   **Equator**   **degrees**
             Southern Hemisphere   **latitude**

Write the word on the line that makes each sentence true.

1. The Equator divides the globe into the _____

   _____ and the _____ .

2. The _____ is at 0° latitude.

Map Check

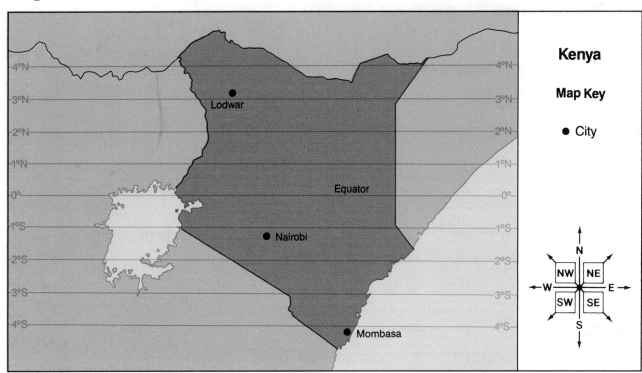

1. Trace the 3°N latitude line in green.

   What city is near that line? _____

2. Trace the 1°S latitude line in orange.

   What city is near that line? _____

3. Trace the 4°S latitude line in red.

   What city is near that line? _____

8 Longitude

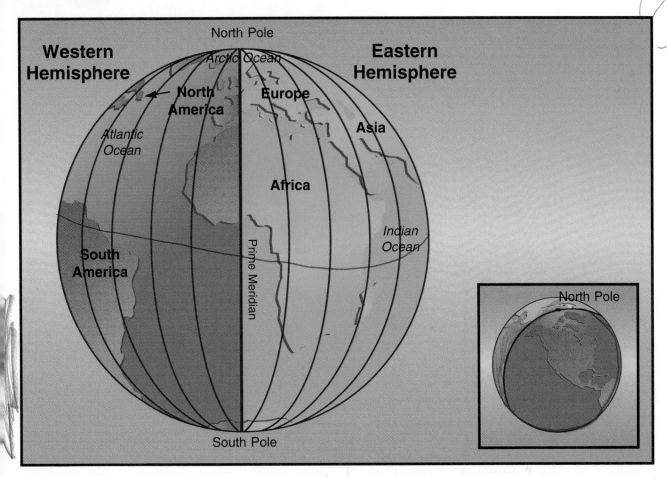

Western Hemisphere

Eastern Hemisphere

North Pole

Arctic Ocean

North America

Europe

Asia

Atlantic Ocean

Africa

Indian Ocean

South America

Prime Meridian

South Pole

North Pole

Another important line on the globe is the **Prime Meridian.** It is an imaginary line that goes from the North Pole to the South Pole.

Find the Prime Meridian in both pictures above. The Prime Meridian divides the globe into two hemispheres. Half the globe east of the Prime Meridian is the **Eastern Hemisphere.** Half the globe west of the Prime Meridian is the **Western Hemisphere.**

► Find the land in the Eastern Hemisphere.
It is colored green.
What continents are in the Eastern Hemisphere?
What oceans are in the Eastern Hemisphere?

► Find the land in the Western Hemisphere.
It is colored brown.
You can see part of three continents. What are they?
What oceans are in the Western Hemisphere?

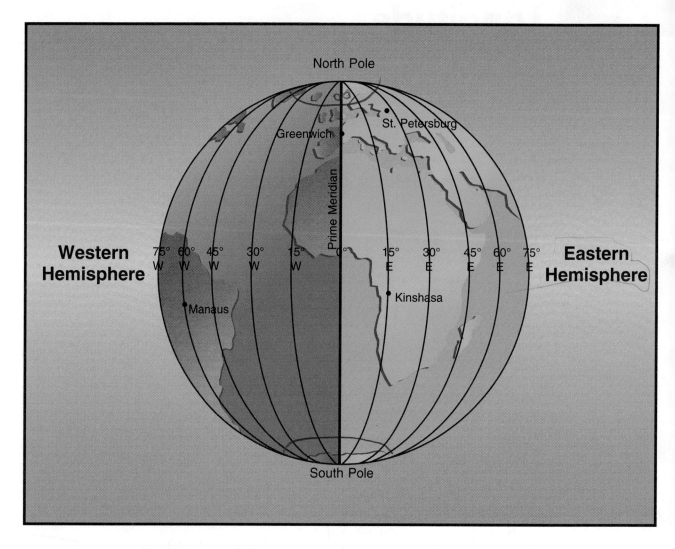

Find the Prime Meridian on the globe above. Now find the curved lines on each side of the Prime Meridian. These are called **lines of longitude**. Why are these lines curved?

We use lines of longitude to locate places east and west of the Prime Meridian. The lines are numbered and marked by degrees. The symbol ° stands for degrees. The Prime Meridian is at 0° longitude.

► Find the 15°E longitude line.
  What does the letter E stand for?
  What city is at 15°East?

► Find the 60°W longitude line.
  What does the letter W stand for?
  What city is at 60°West?

► Find St. Petersburg.
  What line of longitude is it near?

Finding Longitude

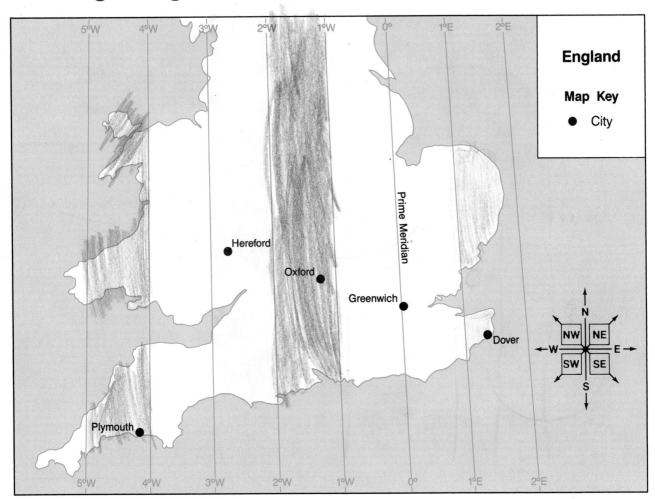

This map shows part of England.

1. Color England green between 1°E and 2°E.

   What city lies in that area? _Dover_

2. Color England brown between 1°W and 2°W.

   What city lies in that area? _Oxford_

3. Color England yellow between 2°W and 3°W.

   What city lies in that area? _hereford_

4. Color England orange between 4°W and 5°W.

   What city lies in that area? _plymouth_

5. What city lies on the Prime Meridian? _Greenwich_

Finding Longitude

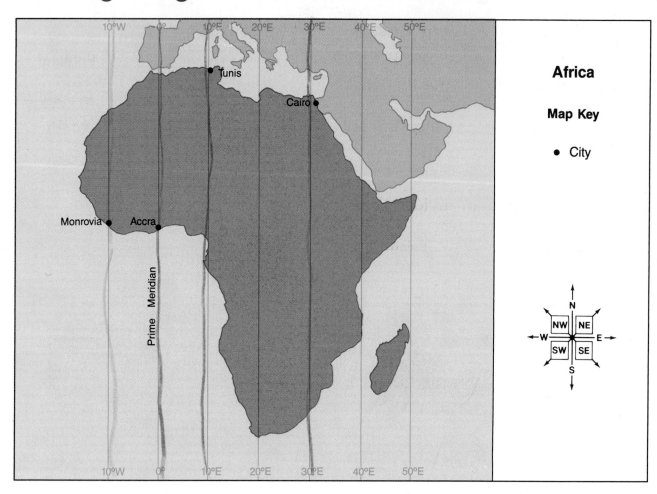

You can find a place if you know which line of longitude it is on.

Study the map of Africa above.

1. Find the Prime Meridian. Trace it in red.

   What city is on the Prime Meridian? _Accra_

2. Find the 10°West line of longitude. Trace it in green.

   What city is at 10°West? _Monrovia_

3. Find the 10°East line of longitude. Trace it in purple.

   What city is at 10°East? _Tunis_

4. Find the 30°East line of longitude. Trace it in orange.

   What city is near 30°East? _Cairo_

Skill Check

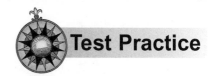 **Test Practice**

Word Check   **Eastern Hemisphere**   **Prime Meridian**
              Western Hemisphere   **lines of longitude**

Write the word on the line that makes each sentence true.

1. _____ measure how far east or west a place is.

2. The _____ is at 0° longitude.

3. The Prime Meridian divides the globe into the _____

_____ and the _____ .

Map Check

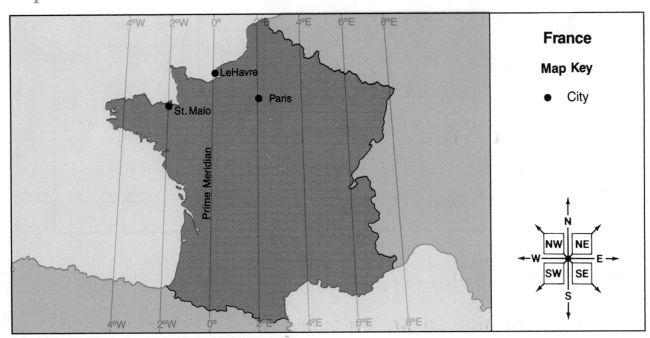

1. Trace the Prime Meridian in green.

   What city is on that line? _____

2. Trace the 2°W longitude line in orange.

   What city is on that line? _____

3. Trace the 2°E longitude line in red.

   What city is on that line? _____

Geography Themes Up Close

Location describes where places are found. You can tell the location of a place by what it is near or what is around it. The map below shows Gabon, a country in Africa.

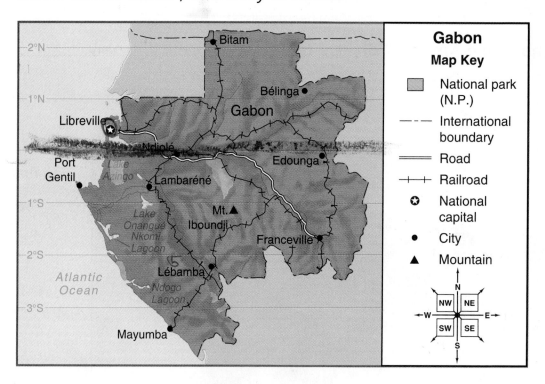

1. Find the Equator (0°) on the map. Trace it in red. What cities are located nearest to the Equator?

   NDJOLE and Edounga

2. Find the capital city of Libreville on the map. Circle it. Describe the location of Libreville.

   Near Railroad.

3. What point of interest is located between 0° and 2° S latitude?

   Port Gentil

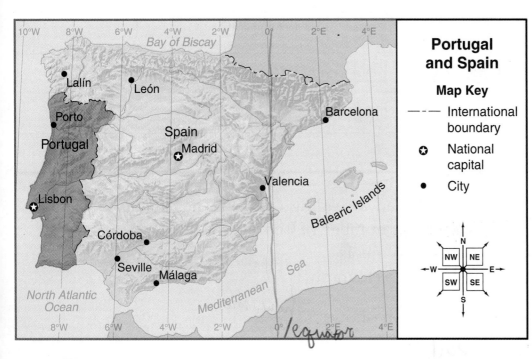

4. Trace the 0° longitude line in green on the map. What is another name for this line of longitude? Add this name to the map.

Equator

5. What line of longitude is nearest to Madrid, Spain?

_4°W_

6. Find the capital of Portugal. Name this city and the line of longitude it is near.

Lisbon

7. Which city in Spain is nearest to the Prime Meridian, Valencia or Barcelona?

_8_

8. Which city in Spain is located near 8°W longitude?

It is Lalin.

9 Graphs

Books Read During Room 10's Reading Contest
📖 stands for one book

Diego ✓	📖 📖 📖 📖 📖 📖
Sarah ⋂	📖 📖 📖 📖 📖
Ayako ʃ	📖 📖 📖 📖
Sam uel	📖 📖

Some students in Room 10 had a reading contest. They made a **pictograph** to keep track of the number of books they read. A pictograph shows facts using symbols.

Follow these steps to read a pictograph.

1. Read the title. This pictograph shows _how many books were read_.

2. Read the key. Each symbol on this graph stands for _one book_.

3. Read the words at the left of the graph. Who read books in this contest? _Diego_ _Sarah_ _Ayako_ _Samuel_

4. Read the longest row of symbols first. Diego read _6_ books.

5. Read the other rows. Write the number of books each student read. Sarah _5_ Ayako _4_ Sam _2_

6. Compare the rows. Use more or fewer.

   Sarah read _1 more_ books than Ayako.

   Sam read _3 less_ books than Sarah.

   Diego read _2 more_ books than Ayako.

Aluminum Cans Collected at Mendez School
▯ stands for 10 pounds of aluminum cans

Second Grade	▯ ▯ ▯
Third Grade	▯ ▯ ▯ ▯ ▯ ▯
Fourth Grade	▯ ▯ ▯ ▯
Fifth Grade	▯ ▯ ▯ ▯
Sixth Grade	▯ ▯ ▯ ▯ ▯

Students at Mendez School were raising money for a new playscape. They collected aluminum cans to sell at the recycling center. They made a pictograph to keep track of the pounds of cans they collected. Follow these steps to finish the pictograph.

1. This pictograph will show _How many pounds of_ _alminium cans Mendez school collected_.

2. Each symbol will stand for _10 Pounds_.

3. The groups who collected cans are the _2nd Grade_, _3rd grade_, _4th grade_, _5th grade_, and _Sixth_.

4. Finish the pictograph. Here are the pounds of cans each grade collected:

Second Grade	30	Fifth Grade	40
Third Grade	60	Sixth Grade	50
Fourth Grade	40		

   Draw one symbol for every 10 pounds of aluminum cans.

5. Compare the rows. The most cans were collected by the _3rd Grade_. The fewest cans were collected by the _2nd Grade_. The _Fourth_ and the _Fifth_ collected the same amount of cans.

Reading a Bar Graph

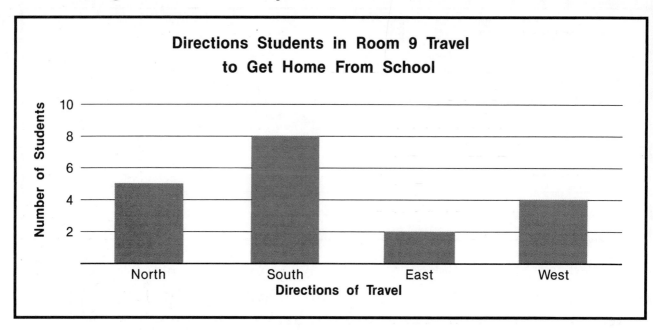

**Directions Students in Room 9 Travel
to Get Home From School**

Number of Students

North   South   East   West

Directions of Travel

The students in Room 9 travel in several directions to get home from school. This bar graph shows how many students go in each direction. A **bar graph** is a graph that uses bars to stand for numbers. Follow these steps to read and use a bar graph.

1. Read the title. This bar graph shows _Directions of travel_

_____ .

2. Read the words at the bottom of each bar. The bars on this graph show _North South East West_ .

3. Read the words and numbers at the left side of the graph.

   Each number on the graph stands for _Students_ .

4. Read the tallest bar. Put your finger at the top of the bar. Move it across the line to the left. Read the number there.

   _8_ people go south to get home from school.

5. How many go north? _5_ west? _4_ east? _2_

6. Compare the bars. Most of the students in Room 9 go _South_

   to get home. The fewest students go _East_ .

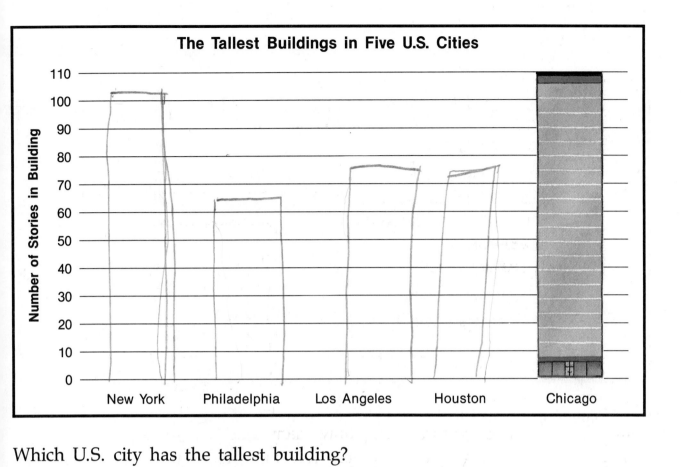

The Tallest Buildings in Five U.S. Cities

Number of Stories in Building

New York   Philadelphia   Los Angeles   Houston   Chicago

Which U.S. city has the tallest building?
Follow these steps to finish this bar graph.

1. This bar graph will show ___The Talled Building___

_____.

2. The bars on this graph will show buildings in the cities of
___NY___, ___Philadelfia___, ___Los La___,
___Houston___, and ___Chicago___.

3. The tallest building in Chicago has ___110___ stories.

4. Finish the graph. Here are the number of stories in each city's
   tallest building: Philadelphia 61; Los Angeles 73;
   Houston 75; New York 102.

5. Compare the bars. The shortest of these buildings is in

   ___Philadelfia___. The two tallest buildings are in
   ___NY ~~Chicago~~___ and ___Chicago___.

Reading a Circle Graph

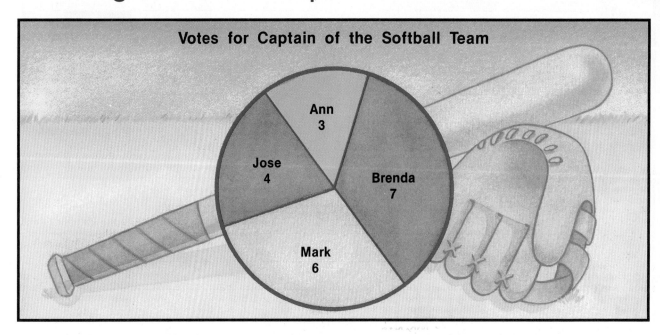

Votes for Captain of the Softball Team

Ann
3

Jose
4

Brenda
7

Mark
6

Four people wanted to be captain of the softball team. The team took a vote. This circle graph shows how the votes were divided. A **circle graph** shows how something whole is divided into parts. Follow these steps to read and use a circle graph.
Finish each step.

1. <u>Read the title.</u> The whole circle stands for <u>Votes for Captain of</u>

   <u>the Softball team</u>   .

2. <u>Read the biggest part of the circle.</u> Who received the most

   votes? <u>Brenda</u>

3. <u>Read the other pieces of the circle.</u> Read clockwise around the circle from the biggest piece. The pieces get smaller as you go.

   Who received the fewest votes? <u>Ann</u>

4. <u>Compare the pieces.</u> To be team captain, the winner has to receive at least half the votes.

   How many votes were there in all? <u>20</u>

   Did anyone receive half of the votes? <u>No</u>

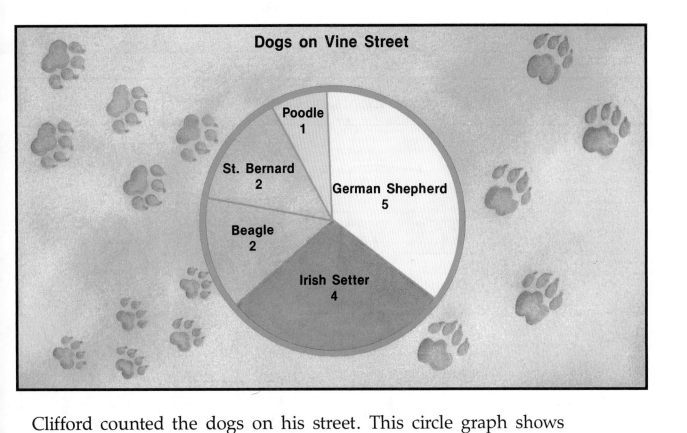

Dogs on Vine Street

Clifford counted the dogs on his street. This circle graph shows how many of each kind of dog he counted.

1. <u>Read the title.</u> The whole circle stands for _Dogs on Vine Street_

_____ .

2. <u>Read the biggest part of the circle.</u> There are more

German Shepards than any other kind of dog.

<u>Read the other pieces of the circle.</u> Read clockwise around the circle from the biggest piece.

3. There is the same number of _St. Bernards_ and

Beagles .

<u>Compare the pieces.</u> Finish each sentence. Use <u>more</u> or <u>fewer</u>.

4. There are _fewer_ poodles than any other dog.

5. There are _less_ St. Bernards than German shepherds.

6. _More_ Irish setters live on Vine Street than beagles.

Reading a Time Line

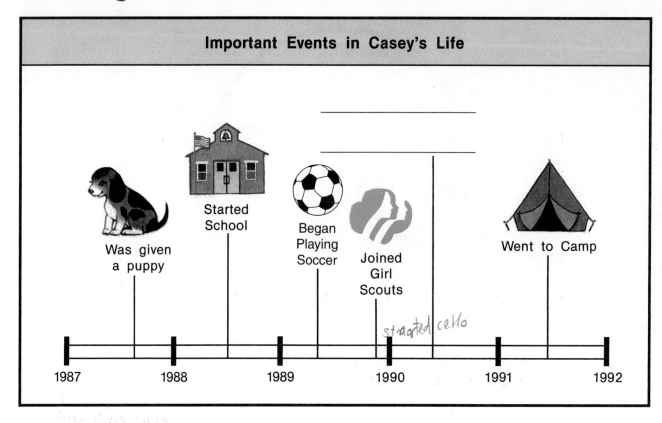

Important Events in Casey's Life

Was given a puppy

Started School

Began Playing Soccer

Joined Girl Scouts

started cello

Went to Camp

1987   1988   1989   1990   1991   1992

A **time line** is a line that shows a number of years. Marks on the line stand for events, or things that happened, during those years. The events are marked in the order they happened. Follow these steps to read a time line.

1. <u>Read the title.</u> This time line shows <u>*Important events in Casey's life*</u>.

2. <u>Read the dates along the bottom of the time line.</u> This time line begins in <u>*1987*</u> and ends in <u>*1992*</u>.

3. <u>Study the order of events on the time line.</u> Write <u>before</u> or <u>after</u>.

   Casey went to camp <u>*after*</u> she got a puppy.

   Casey began to play soccer <u>*before*</u> she joined Girl Scouts.

4. <u>Add to the time line.</u> In 1990 Casey started cello lessons. Write "Started cello lessons" on the line in 1990.

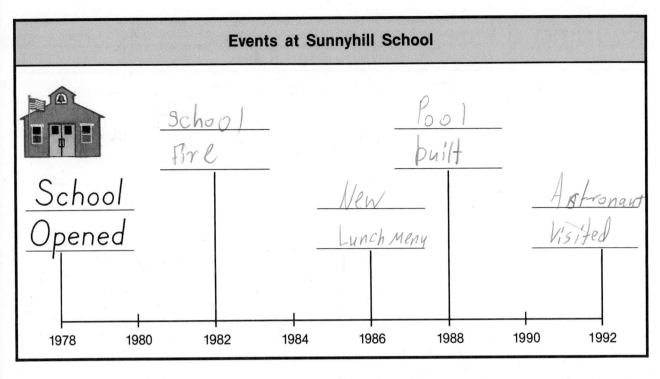

Events at Sunnyhill School

School Fire

Pool built

School Opened

New Lunch Meny

Astronaut Visited

| 1978 | 1980 | 1982 | 1984 | 1986 | 1988 | 1990 | 1992 |

Casey is writing a report about things that happened at her school since it opened in 1978. She wants to show them on a time line. Follow the steps to finish the time line.

1. Read the title. This time line shows _Events at Sunny hill Scool_

2. Read the dates along the bottom of the time line. This

   time line begins in _1978_ and ends in _1992_ .

3. Put the events in order. Number these events from 1 to 5, in the order they happened.

   _____ 1988 New lunch menu

   _____ 1982 School caught fire

   _____ 1992 Astronaut visited

   _____ 1986 Pool built

   _____ 1978 School opened

4. Write the events in order on the time line. Write each event on the line above the year it happened. The first event is written for you.

Reading a Line Graph

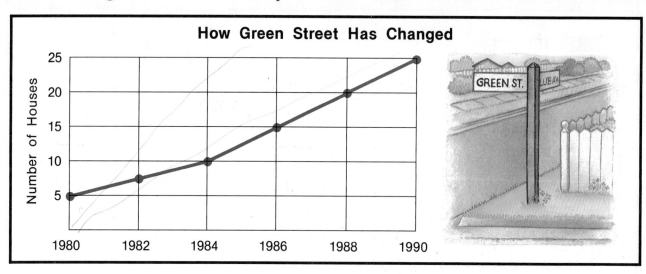

How Green Street Has Changed

A **line graph** can show how something changes over time. This line graph shows how the number of houses on Green Street changed. Follow these steps to read a line graph.

1. Read the title. This line graph shows _How green Street has changed._

2. Read the dates along the bottom of the graph. Read from left to right. This graph shows how things changed between the years of _1980_ and _1990_.

3. Read the words and numbers on the left side of the graph. The numbers stand for _Number of houses_.

4. Read the dots on the line. Put your finger on the dot above 1980. Slide it to the left to read the number of houses on Green Street that year.

   In 1980 there were _5_ houses on Green Street.

   In 1984 there were _10_ houses on Green Street.

5. Study the shape of the line. Does it go up or down? The line shows that the number of houses on Green Street has grown _Greater_ every year since 1980.
   greater/smaller

Read your book

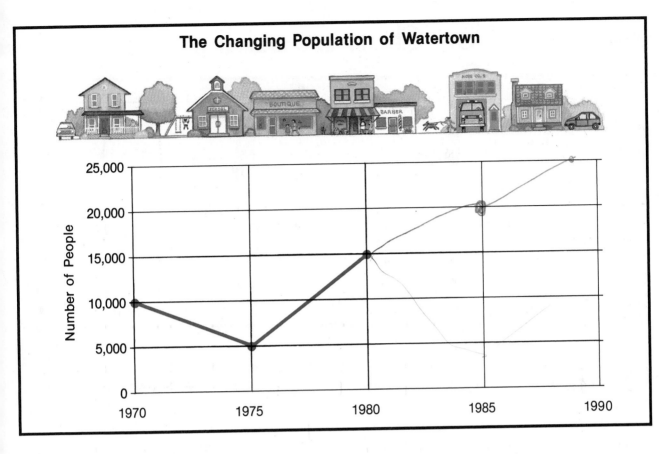

The Changing Population of Watertown

This line graph shows how the population of Watertown has changed over time. Follow the steps to finish the line graph. How has the population changed?

1. This line graph shows _Changing Population of Water town_.

2. This graph will show how the population changed between

   the years of _1970_ and _1980_.

3. In 1970 there were _10,000_ people in Watertown.

   In 1975 there were _5,000_. In 1980 there were _15,000_.

4. <u>Finish the line.</u> In 1985 the population was 20,000. In 1990 the population was 25,000. Add dots for 1985 and 1990. Connect the dots to complete the line.

5. Did the population of Watertown grow greater or smaller

   between 1975 and 1990? _Greater_

Reading a Flow Chart

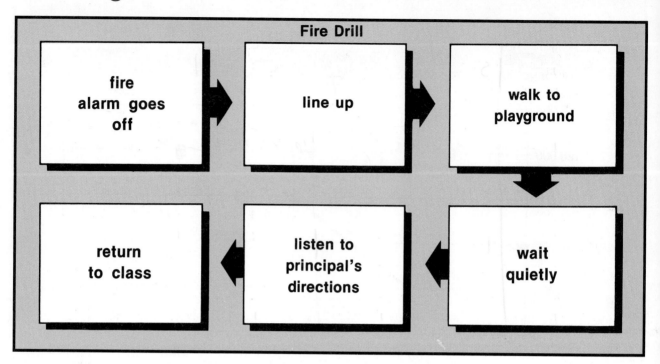

Fire Drill

fire alarm goes off → line up → walk to playground → wait quietly → listen to principal's directions → return to class

Suppose your school is having a fire drill. To be safe, you must follow some important steps. A **flow chart** is a drawing that shows the steps for doing or making something. Follow these steps to read a flow chart.

1. Read the title. This flow chart shows the steps for _a fire drill_
   fire alarm goes off.

2. Read the steps. Follow the arrows. Start at the top left
   corner. The first step in the fire drill is _fire alarm goes off._

   The last step is _Wa return to class_.

3. Study the order of the steps.
   Walk to the playground before you _Wait quielly_.
   Line up after _you fire alarm goes of_.
   Listen to the principal's directions after you _wait_.
   Walk to the playground after you _____.

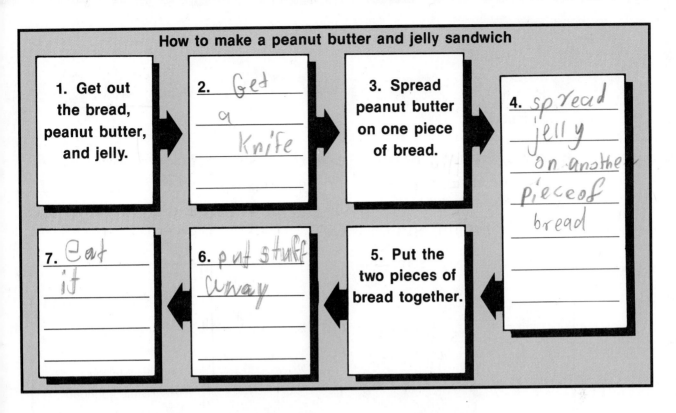

How to make a peanut butter and jelly sandwich

1. Get out the bread, peanut butter, and jelly.

2. _Get a Knife_

3. Spread peanut butter on one piece of bread.

4. _spread jelly on another piece of bread_

5. Put the two pieces of bread together.

6. _put stuff away_

7. _Eat it_

Some of the steps have been left out of this flow chart. Follow the directions to read and finish it.

1. This flow chart shows how to _Make a Sandwich_ .

2. The first step in making a peanut butter and jelly sandwich is to _Get out materials_ .

3. Add these missing steps to the flow chart above.
   (2.) Get a knife.
   (4.) Spread jelly on another piece of bread.
   (6.) Put everything away.
   (7.) Eat it!

4. Study the order of the steps.
   Before you put the two pieces of bread together you must
   Spread jelly .

   The last step in making a peanut butter and jelly sandwich is to _Eat It!_ .

Geography Themes Up Close

Human/Environment Interaction describes how people live in their environment. The environment has resources people can use. Where there is rich soil, people can farm. People use rivers and lakes for water, for fun, and for travel.

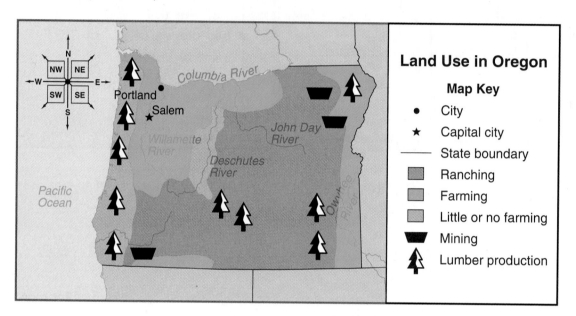

1. Where is most of the farming done in Oregon?

   In the north West by the Willamette

2. In what parts of Oregon do people grow trees for lumber?

   East and South

3. Where is mining done in Oregon?

   NW and SE

4. Write a sentence that describes how people in Oregon live in their environment.

   Ranch Farm Mine Lumbue

Events at Lake Ellyn

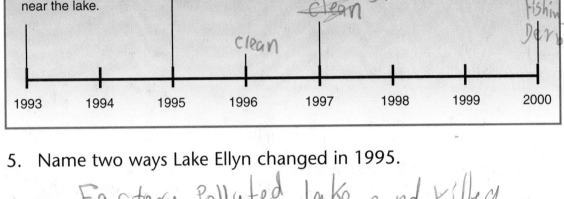

Factory was built near the lake.

Factory polluted lake and killed fish.

New fish
clean

clean

Fishing Derby

1993 1994 1995 1996 1997 1998 1999 2000

5. Name two ways Lake Ellyn changed in 1995.

> Factory Polluted lake and killed fish

6. Add the following events to the time line. Write each event in order on the time line.

In 2000 Lake Ellyn held a fishing derby.
In 1996 Lake Ellyn was cleaned.
In 1997 new fish were put into Lake Ellyn.

7. Look at the time line. Explain one way people changed the environment of Lake Ellyn.

So fish was healthy.

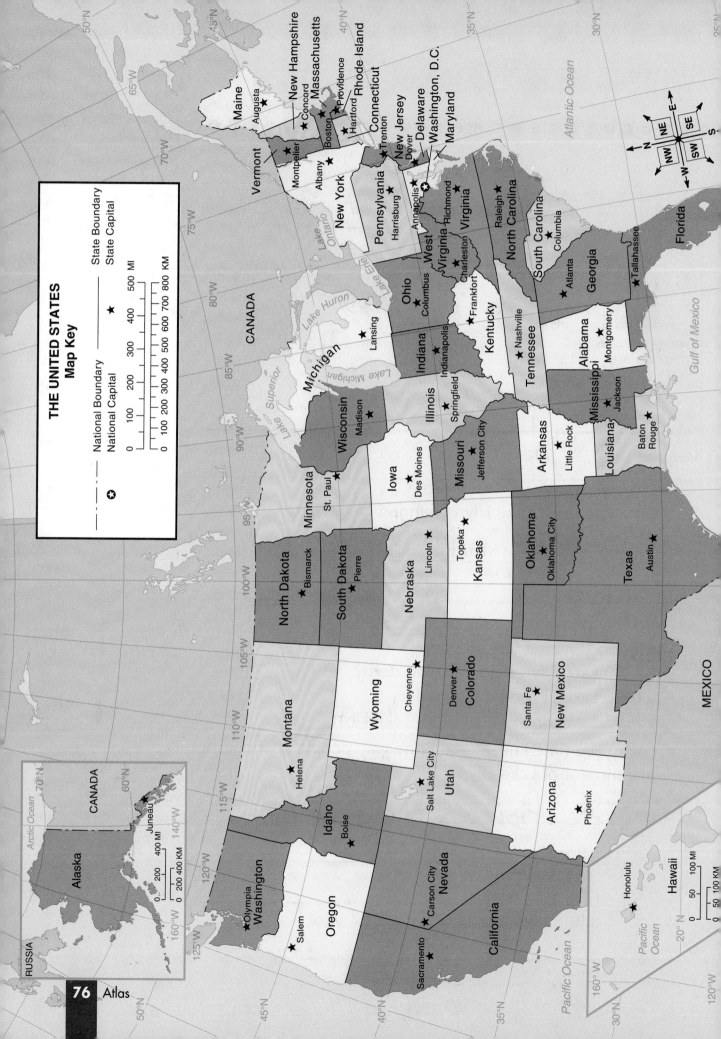

THE UNITED STATES
Map Key

National Boundary
State Boundary

National Capital ✪
State Capital ★

MI
0 100 200 300 400 500
0 100 200 300 400 500 600 700 800 KM

Maine · Augusta

New Hampshire · Concord

Massachusetts · Boston

Providence · Hartford

Rhode Island

Connecticut

New Jersey · Trenton

Delaware · Dover

Washington, D.C.

Maryland · Annapolis

Vermont · Montpelier

New York · Albany

Pennsylvania · Harrisburg

West Virginia · Charleston

Virginia · Richmond

North Carolina · Raleigh

South Carolina · Columbia

Florida · Tallahassee

Ohio · Columbus

Kentucky · Frankfort

Tennessee · Nashville

Georgia · Atlanta

Alabama · Montgomery

Michigan · Lansing

Indiana · Indianapolis

Illinois · Springfield

Mississippi · Jackson

Wisconsin · Madison

Missouri · Jefferson City

Arkansas · Little Rock

Louisiana · Baton Rouge

Minnesota · St. Paul

Iowa · Des Moines

North Dakota · Bismarck

South Dakota · Pierre

Nebraska · Lincoln

Kansas · Topeka

Oklahoma · Oklahoma City

Texas · Austin

Montana · Helena

Wyoming · Cheyenne

Colorado · Denver

New Mexico · Santa Fe

Idaho · Boise

Utah · Salt Lake City

Arizona · Phoenix

Nevada · Carson City

California · Sacramento

Washington · Olympia

Oregon · Salem

CANADA

MEXICO

RUSSIA

Atlantic Ocean

Gulf of Mexico

Pacific Ocean

Arctic Ocean

Lake Superior

Lake Michigan

Lake Huron

Lake Erie

Lake Ontario

Alaska
CANADA
RUSSIA
Juneau ★
Arctic Ocean
MI
0   200   400
0 200 400 KM

Hawaii
Honolulu ★
MI
0   50   100
0   50 100 KM

70°N · 80°N · 80°N · 70°N

180° · 0°

160°W · 40°W

Arctic Ocean · 140°W · 20°W

120°W · 100°W · 80°W · 60°W

Greenland

60°N

(U.S.)

50°N

Canada · *Hudson Bay*

Pacific Ocean

⭐ Ottawa · 40°N

Great Lakes

United States

⭐ Washington, D.C. · *Atlantic Ocean*

30°N

Mexico · *Gulf of Mexico*

Bahamas

U.S. Virgin Islands · 20°N

Cuba

Haiti · Puerto Rico

⭐ Mexico City · Dominican Republic

Jamaica

Belize · *Caribbean Sea*

Guatemala · Honduras

El Salvador · Nicaragua · 10°N

Costa Rica · Panama

Compass rose:
N
NW NE
W E
SW SE
S

NORTH AMERICA

0   200   400   600 MI

0   200 400 600 800 KM

120°W · 110°W · 100°W · 90°W · 80°W · 70°W

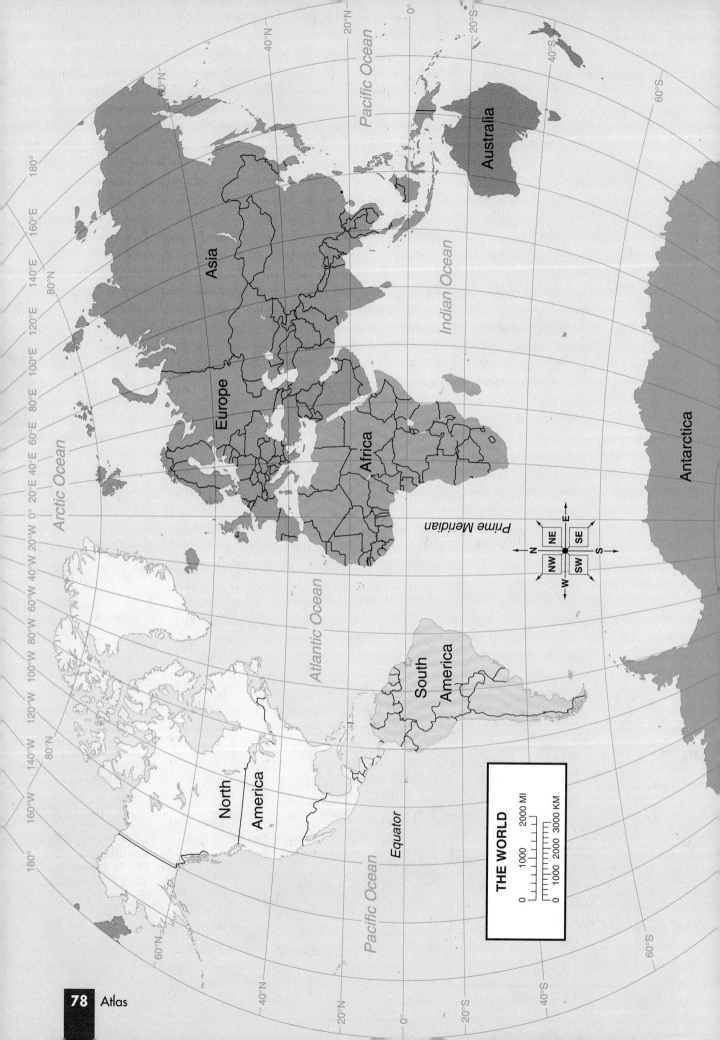

THE WORLD

Pacific Ocean

20°N · 40°N · 80°N · 60°N

Arctic Ocean

Asia

Europe

Africa

Prime Meridian

Indian Ocean

Australia

Antarctica

Atlantic Ocean

South America

North America

Equator

Pacific Ocean

N
NW · NE
W · E
SW · SE
S

0   1000   2000 MI
0   1000   2000   3000 KM

Glossary

bar graph (p. 64)   a graph with thick lines, or bars, of different lengths to compare numbers or amounts

circle graph (p. 66)   a circle that shows how something whole is divided into parts

coast (p. 28)   the land next to the ocean

compass rose (p. 8)   a symbol that shows the directions: north, south, east, and west

continent (p. 50)   a very large body of land

degrees (p. 51)   the unit of measurement used for lines of latitude and longitude

distance (p. 14)   how far one place is from another

Eastern Hemisphere (p. 55) the half of Earth east of the Prime Meridian

environment (p. 5)   the land, water, and air around you. It is the plant and animal life, too.

Equator (p. 50)   the imaginary line that goes around the middle of Earth. The Equator divides Earth into the Northern and Southern Hemispheres.

factory (p. 22)   a place where resources are made into other things

flow chart (p. 72)   a drawing that shows steps for doing or making something

geography (p. 4)   about Earth and how people live and work on Earth

grid (p. 42)   a pattern of lines that cross each other to form squares

gulf (p. 28)   a large body of water that cuts deep into the land

hemisphere (p. 50)   half of the globe or half of Earth. The four hemispheres are Northern, Southern, Eastern, and Western.

human/environment interaction (p. 5, 74)   explains how people live in their environment

human features (p. 4)   things such as houses, roads, bridges, schools, farms, and factories that people make

intermediate directions (p. 11) northeast, southeast, southwest, northwest

interstate highway (p. 38)   a highway that crosses the entire country

kilometers (p. 14)   a metric unit of length for measuring distance. Also written **KM** and km.

landform map (p. 28)   a map that shows the shape of the land, such as mountains and hills

line graph (p. 70)   a graph that shows how something changes over time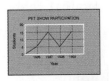

lines of latitude (p. 51) lines that circle Earth north and south of the Equator. They are numbered and marked by degrees.

lines of longitude (p. 56) lines that circle Earth from the North Pole to the South Pole. They are numbered and marked by degrees.

location (p. 4, 60) tells where something can be found

map (p. 8) a drawing of a real place

map index (p. 43) the alphabetical list of places on a map with their grid squares

map key (p. 8) the guide to what the symbols on a map stand for

map scale (p. 14) the guide to what the distances on a map stand for

miles (p. 14) a unit of length used in measuring distance. Also written **MI** or mi.

mountain range (p. 31) a group or chain of mountains

movement (p. 6, 48) describes how people, goods, information, and ideas get from place to place

Northern Hemisphere (p. 50) the half of Earth north of the Equator

physical features (p. 4) are things from nature, such as bodies of water, landforms, weather, plants, and animals

pictograph (p. 62) a way to show and compare facts using symbols

place (p. 4, 20) tells what a location is like

plains (p. 28) large areas of flat lands

plateau (p. 28) high, flat land

Prime Meridian (p. 55) the line of longitude from the South Pole to the North Pole measured at 0°. It divides Earth into Eastern and Western Hemispheres.

regions (p. 7, 34) areas that have something in common

resources (p. 22) things people can use, such as oil, lumber, and water

route (p. 36) a road or path from one place to another. Highways, railroads, and trails are routes.

Southern Hemisphere (p. 50) the half of Earth south of the Equator

state highway (p. 38) a main road that connects cities and towns within the boundaries of one state

symbol (p. 8) a picture on a map that stands for something real

time line (p. 68) a line that shows a number of years and the events that happened in order

U.S. highway (p. 37) a main highway that passes through more than one state

Western Hemisphere (p. 55) the half of Earth west of the Prime Meridian